Contributions to Finance and Accounting

The book series 'Contributions to Finance and Accounting' features the latest research from research areas like financial management, investment, capital markets, financial institutions, FinTech and financial innovation, accounting methods and standards, reporting, and corporate governance, among others. Books published in this series are primarily monographs and edited volumes that present new research results, both theoretical and empirical, on a clearly defined topic. All books are published in print and digital formats and disseminated globally.

This book series is indexed in Scopus.

Dawei Zhao · Jia Yuan · Wei Chen

FinTech and SupTech in China

Springer

Dawei Zhao
Research Institute
People's Bank of China
Beijing, China

Jia Yuan
Research Institute
People's Bank of China
Beijing, China

Wei Chen
Asset Management
Fangda Partners
Shanghai, China

ISSN 2730-6038 ISSN 2730-6046 (electronic)
Contributions to Finance and Accounting
ISBN 978-981-99-5172-7 ISBN 978-981-99-5173-4 (eBook)
https://doi.org/10.1007/978-981-99-5173-4

This Springer imprint is published by the registered company Springer Nature Singapore Pte Ltd.
The registered company address is: 152 Beach Road, #21-01/04 Gateway East, Singapore 189721, Singapore

Preface

With government support, increasing consumer demand, and a rapidly expanding technology sector, FinTech (Financial Technology) and SupTech (Supervisory Technology) are growing rapidly in China.

China is one of the largest FinTech markets in the world, with a total transaction value of USD 29.5 trillion in 2019. The Chinese government has actively promoted the development of FinTech, with policies aimed at supporting innovation and creating a more inclusive financial system. China's most popular FinTech services include mobile payments, online lending, and wealth management. The dominant players in the Chinese FinTech market are Alipay and WeChat Pay, which have created highly integrated ecosystems offering a wide range of financial services. Regulators in China have also taken steps to ensure the safety and stability of the FinTech industry, with new regulations on data privacy, risk management, and capital requirements.

SupTech refers to using technology to enhance regulatory oversight and improve compliance in the financial sector. China has been a leader in SupTech development, with a number of initiatives aimed at improving regulatory efficiency and effectiveness. For example, the People's Bank of China (the "PBOC") has established a FinTech development plan that includes SupTech as a critical priority. The China Securities Regulatory Commission (the "CSRC") has also established a regulatory sandbox to test and develop new SupTech applications. China's most promising SupTech tools include Natural Language Processing (NLP), machine learning, and Big Data analytics, which can help regulators detect and prevent financial crimes, monitor systemic risk, and improve regulatory transparency.

The growth of FinTech and SupTech in China has been driven by a combination of government support, consumer demand, and technological innovation. As these fields continue to evolve, they are likely to play an increasingly important role in shaping the future of China's financial system.

Beijing, China Dawei Zhao
Beijing, China Jia Yuan
Shanghai, China Wei Chen

Contents

About the Authors

Dawei Zhao Ph.D. in Economics is currently the Senior Research Fellow in the Research Institute of the People's Bank of China. He holds Bachelor, Master, and Doctorate degree of economics all from Central University of Finance and Economics. He has won the First Award of the "Youth Research Project" of the People's Bank of China (2019, 2020), the First Award of the "2017–2018 the PBC FinTech Research Project" by FinTech Committee of the People's Bank of China, and the First Award of the "2018 FinTech Youth Thesis" by FinTech Research Center of National Institution for Finance & Development. With a long-term focus on FinTech and RegTech, he has published more than 70 academic papers. As the author and co-author, he has compiled "Artificial Financial Intelligence in China", "The Era of Intelligent Finance", "Technology Driven Innovation: Digital Transformation in Private Equity", "Technology Rebuild Finance: FinTech Utilization and Perspective", "Chained Future: Blockchain Theory and Application", "China FinTech Annual Report (2018, 2019, 2020, 2021, 2022)", "Annual Report on China's RegTech Development (2019, 2020, 2021)", and other works.

Jia Yuan Ph.D. in Economics is currently the Senior Research Fellow in the Research Institute of the People's Bank of China. He holds Master and Doctorate degree of economics from University of International Business and Economics in China, and as a Visiting Scholar in Indiana University in 2011 in the US. His research focuses on international economics and finance, macroeconomics and fintech. Dozens of his academic papers and articles have been published in top domestic journals such as Journal of Financial Research, and he has a book named "Globalization Dividend and the Changing Distribution of Income".

Wei Chen graduated from UIBE with a Master's degree in law. He now works at Fangda Partners and once served in the People's Bank of China. His research interests lie primarily in asset management and FinTech. He has published multiple articles in CSSCI journal, Financial News, China Banking and Insurance News, and some other national academic journals. He has presided over a youth academic project of the PBOC Shanghai Head Office in 2019 and an academic project of the

Shanghai Society of Finance in 2020. With rich experience in asset management, he has provided legal services on data governance and data protection for internationally renowned hedge funds, joint venture fund companies, banking financial institutions, FinTech companies, and wealth management companies.

Part I
FinTech in China

FinTech has experienced explosive growth in China over the past decade, driven by many factors, including a large population of tech-savvy consumers, government support for innovation, and a rapidly expanding middle class. This market includes various financial services such as mobile payments, online lending, and digital wealth management. Furthermore, the growth of FinTech in China has also been driven by government support for innovation in financial services.

- **Mobile payments**: Mobile payments are ubiquitous in China, with services like Alipay and WeChat Pay dominating the market. These platforms allow users to pay for everything from groceries to rent using smartphones.
- **Online lending**: Online lending platforms have become increasingly popular in China, particularly among small- and medium-sized enterprises (SMEs) with difficulty accessing traditional bank loans. Many of these platforms use data-driven algorithms to assess creditworthiness and offer quick loans at competitive rates.
- **Wealth management**: FinTech has also disrupted the wealth management industry in China, with platforms like Ant Group's Yu'e Bao and Tencent's Licaitong offering investment opportunities to individuals with small amounts of capital.
- **Regulatory environment**: The Chinese government has supported FinTech innovation and closely regulates the industry. In 2020, the government suspended the IPO of Ant Group, a major FinTech player, due to concerns over the company's size and risk management practices.

FinTech has transformed the financial landscape in China, making it easier and more convenient for consumers and businesses to access financial services. However, the industry also faces challenges related to regulation and risk management, as well as potential competition from traditional financial institutions.

Part I
FinTech in China

Chapter 1
Overview of FinTech

Introduction

Generally, FinTech refers to applying emerging technologies represented by Artificial Intelligence (AI), Blockchain, Cloud Computing, and Big Data in the financial sector. FinTech combines data and technology innovation with financial business scenarios. In the past years, FinTech's broad and in-depth applications in the financial sector around various countries have given birth to new financial services, financial organizations, and financial models, posing multiple complex and challenging regulatory tasks to regulators worldwide and their traditional regulatory methods. For the healthy growth of the financial market, financial regulators need to encourage and regulate FinTech at an appropriate balance. Therefore, their first step is to clearly understand what FinTech is and what risks FinTech might bring (Lu and Yao 2015).

As early as the year 2016, the Financial Stability Board (the "FSB") defined FinTech as technologically enabled innovation in financial services that could result in new business models, applications, processes, or products with an associated material effect on financial markets and institutions and the provision of financial services. FinTech innovations are affecting many different areas of financial services.[1]

In China, the PBOC has been making great efforts to research, regulate and encourage the development and application of FinTech. On August 22, 2019, the PBOC issued the FinTech Development Plan (2019–2021), in which the PBOC follows FSB's definition of FinTech and further explains that such a definition has been widely recognized around the globe.[2]

Furthermore, on January 4, 2022, the PBOC issued the FinTech Development Plan (2022–2025) based on China's legislative and market practices from 2019 to 2021. On March 12, 2021, the National People's Congress of the People's Republic of China issued the Outline of the 14th Five-Year Plan (2021–2025) for National Economic and Social Development and Long-Range Objectives for 2035.

---

[1] https://www.fsb.org/work-of-the-fsb/financial-innovation-and-structural-change/fintech/.

[2] http://www.pbc.gov.cn/goutongjiaoliu/113456/113469/3878634/index.html.

D. Zhao et al., *FinTech and SupTech in China*, Contributions to Finance and Accounting,
https://doi.org/10.1007/978-981-99-5173-4_1

1.1 Underlying Technologies of FinTech

From relevant market practices in recent years, FinTech has five underlying technologies: Artificial Intelligence, Blockchain, Cloud Computing, Big Data, and Internet Technology. Internet Technology has been mature for a long time and lays the most basic foundation for FinTech. In contrast, Artificial Intelligence, Blockchain, Cloud Computing, and Big Data are all emerging technologies in recent years. They should be treated more cautiously, as their potential risks to the financial market cannot be fully recognized for the time being.

The financial industry is closely related to technological innovation, concerning frequent financial transactions and intensive financial information storage and exchanges. Therefore, it is easy to understand that finance is one of the industries with the broadest application of FinTech. That being said, finance is an industry highly driven by technological advances due to the close connection between them as determined by their business characteristics and proven by the market practices of various market players (including but not limited to financial institutions) regarding FinTech application (Mo and Zhao 2017).

Financial institutions are active promoters and direct beneficiaries of the emergence and improvement of modern technologies and the promoted financial industry. Financial institutions can widely utilize FinTech to optimize their investment and financing function, insurance function, risk management function, etc. In the course, financial institutions can reduce costs by automating specific processes and attracting more customers. For example, financial institutions can provide tailored financial products or services using Artificial Intelligence. The competitive edge brought by technological advances will be favored by those financial institutions that walk at the forefront of the FinTech market (China Institute of Information and Communications Research 2018).

1.2 Players in the FinTech Market

From the market and regulatory practices, four major players exist in the highly dynamic FinTech market.[3] They are FinTech start-ups, BigTechs, financial institutions, and financial regulators, among which Fintech start-ups and BigTechs are new participants that pose more challenges to the traditional financial regulation system. Considering that effective and efficient financial regulation relies on a comprehensive and profound understanding of market players (regulators included), below, we will discuss the four players mentioned above in detail one by one.

[3] Joint Task Force of China Wealth Management 50 Forum and Tsinghua University Wudaokou School of Finance (Apr 2021) A Study on the Regulation of Platform FinTech Companies.

1.2.1 *FinTech Start-Ups*

FinTech start-ups refer to the technology companies whose Research and Development on FinTech is at an early stage for the time being. A typical FinTech start-up is one with a solid dedication to identifying the pain points in the existing financial business models and the existing financial market. In other words, a FinTech start-up is about providing innovative technical remedies, represented by biometrics and Big Data, to solve problems or difficulties which existing solutions cannot cope with or cannot cope with efficiently and effectively. Furthermore, regarding the business model and target customers, the FinTech start-up can provide services directly to individual customers and provide technical support in the form of products or outsourcing services to financial institutions based on its condition, expectations, market positioning, and the outer environment.

1.2.2 *BigTechs*

The BigTechs are quite competitive in the FinTech market by virtue of their Internet advantages. Nowadays, it is common for BigTechs to enter the financial market by acquiring financial licenses through planned acquisitions. Initially, they might operate in specific business areas like e-commerce, social networking, entertainment, telecommunications, etc. As their business grows, they may accumulate a large customer base from that place. The BigTechs "own" a large amount of data from their specific customer relationships. They might, driven by profit maximization, leverage these data to provide tailored/improved financial services to their existing customers or sell these data to traditional financial institutions and any other subjects willing to pay. Since they are experienced in technology development/application, BigTechs have more nuanced algorithm-related knowledge concerning customer choices and preferences than traditional financial institutions. At an early stage, when most BigTechs were not familiar with financial business or were not ready to engage in the financial market, they might choose to sell their customers' data to traditional financial institutions or become channels for the latter. However, when the timing comes, the BigTechs will prefer to directly provide financial services for their customers by themselves to pursue more profits or make preparations for taking more market share. Some BigTechs also work as vendors to provide technical support, such as cloud services for traditional financial institutions (Huang and Huang 2018).

1.2.3 *Traditional Financial Institutions*

In this book, traditional financial institutions refer to traditional licensed institutions. For now, traditional financial institutions are under severe pressure from emerging financial market participants and customer behavior changes and trying to adapt to and actively rise to this unprecedented technical transformation brought by FinTech. In this process of "battling" with the emerging market players, they develop underlying technologies independently or cooperatively, purchase FinTech Products from their vendors, and explore innovative application scenarios to enhance their efficiency in providing financial services and to improve customer experience by virtue of more intellectual and tailored services.

1.2.4 Financial Regulators

Financial regulators play double roles as referees and players in the FinTech market. Authorized by laws and regulations, financial regulators have a statutory and inescapable responsibility for developing FinTech infrastructures, including payment systems, digital currencies, and credit reporting systems. In Part II, this book will introduce another concept—SupTech, referring to the FinTech leveraged by financial regulators to smooth or improve their regulation and supervision process.

In China, financial regulators are actively utilizing FinTech to monitor targeted entities' compliance status and many other aspects, which promotes the digitization and automation of financial regulation. Financial regulators should "participate" in the FinTech market because, to face the regulatory challenges brought by technological innovations and be qualified regulators in the era of transformation, they should be equipped with cutting-edge knowledge of FinTech, and sufficient talents specialized in Fintech. This book defines the FinTech financial regulators use as "SupTech" for understanding convenience (Andy 2014).

1.3 Artificial Intelligence in the Finance Sector

1.3.1 What is AI?

AI uses computer systems to simulate human thinking processes and their intelligent behaviors represented by learning, reasoning, thinking, and planning. As a result, AI can provide high stability, reduce operational risk and moral hazard, and improve decision-making and transaction efficiency, increasingly attracting attention in the financial sector in recent years.

For now, partially mature AI applications such as Alpha Go and facial recognition could only be viewed as solutions for solving specific problems under specific scenarios. Such AI applications with restricted usages cannot provide depth and breadth solutions. In other words, they cannot solve problems effectively and simultaneously solve problems of various types. In China, most industries' practices in AI applications still need to mature (Du 2018).

For the financial industry, integrating AI technology and specific financial scenarios is still being explored. From our surveys, major AI technologies applied in the financial sector include machine learning, language processing, biometric recognition, and knowledge atlas. In the application process, traditional financial institutions, while facing increasingly fierce inner and outer pressure, concentrate on developing intelligent financial service that improves service efficiency, customer experience, and customer stickiness. Some traditional financial institutions which lack the self-development capacity or consider the cost-effectiveness may prefer to purchase relevant products or technical solutions from external vendors such as FinTech companies, outsource wholly or partially to external vendors, or seek technical support or expert secondments from external vendors. Intelligent financial service includes intelligent marketing, patronage, customer service, and risk control.

However, adding tiny intelligence into the financial service is still far from what we call "AI integration with finance." That being said, there is still a long and thorny way to successfully transform service intelligence into decision intelligence (see Table 1.1).

1.3.2 AI Application in the Financial Sector

FinTech development and FinTech innovation could give birth to AI-centered financial intelligence. Financial intelligence represents higher production efficiency and broader production factors and can be viewed as an achievement in an advanced stage of FinTech development. The AI industry chain comprises three layers: fundamentals, technology and applications. In the fundamental layer, Big Data and Cloud Computing technologies are applied in credit investigation, insurance, payment, etc. (Lin 2017) In the technology layer, machine learning, neural network, and knowledge mapping technologies are applied in investment advisors, intelligent quantitative transactions, credit investigation (Liu 2017), anti-fraud detection, computer vision, and biometric identification. Technologies represented by speech recognition and natural language processing (NLP) are applied to provide intelligent customer service and intelligent investment analysis. Finally, in the application layer, technologies represented by cognitive intelligence are applied in risk control.

The financial industry has built-in advantages in AI applications. For one thing, finance is a data-intensive industry processing and living on a large amount of data. For example, no matter whether traditional players represented by banks, securities companies, and insurance companies, or emerging players represented by Internet financial institutions and FinTech companies, most of them operate their business highly based on customer and market data processing and, therefore would benefit from cross-platform data sharing, super-scale information or data communication and innovations on data related technologies. In turn, their good practices would adversely promote AI applications and AI innovations in the financial sector. For another, continuing the dividends created in the computer and Internet era, emerging

Table 1.1 Internet giants are actively exploring AI application scenarios

	Personal assistant	Search tool	Driverless	Health care	Cloud service	Games	Home furnishing	E-commerce	Finance	Vehicle	Wearable devices	Social networking	Others	Landscape
Google	√	√	√	√	√	√	√			√	√	√		Full deployment
Microsoft	√	√			√									Focus on technology development and Microsoft products customer experience enhancement
Apple	√		√				√			√	√			Focus on Apple products' customer experience enhancement
Amazon	√				√		√	√		√	√		√	Focus on intelligence transformation in home furnishing, cloud services, e-commerce, and retailing business

(continued)

Table 1.1 (continued)

	Personal assistant	Search tool	Driverless	Health care	Cloud service	Games	Home furnishing	E-commerce	Finance	Vehicle	Wearable devices	Social networking	Others	Landscape
Facebook	√	√										√		Focus on Facebook applications customer experience enhancement by AI technology
Baidu	√	√	√	√	√				√	√			√	Full deployment

(continued)

Table 1.1 (continued)

	Personal assistant	Search tool	Driverless	Health care	Cloud service	Games	Home furnishing	E-commerce	Finance	Vehicle	Wearable devices	Social networking	Others	Landscape
Tencent	√	√		√	√	√	√					√		Supported by a complete AI ecology system based on a broad and solid user network. Focus on social networking, games, etc.
Alibaba				√	√		√	√	√	√			√	Supported by Alibaba cloud. Focus on e-commerce, finance, and traditional industries such as transportation and retailing business

innovative technologies and applications thereof, such as data mining, image recognition, natural language processing, speech recognition, and voice print recognition, are on the road to sophistication with the time moved, just as what computer and Internet had gone through in the past decades.

1.3.3 Principles for AI Development and Application

The AI era is approaching and is about to change our lives. How to guide AI to develop securely and legitimately when AI integrates with the financial industry has become a common topic facing financial regulators worldwide. So far, the international community has reached several preliminary consensuses regarding ethics and technical security: as follows. Firstly, subjects developing and applying AI should conform to the values and ethics recognized by human society. That being said, such subjects should be prohibited from destroying the existing social system, structure, and mechanism. Secondly, AI developers and appliers should be able to clearly explain the benefits and decision logic of their AI outputs, which can be effectively comprehended by professional third parties for promotions if needed and can be identified and corrected by them if any mistakes. Thirdly, AI developers and appliers should be kept accountable for their decisions and actions related to AI. That being said, their decisions and actions related to AI should be traceable for continuous supervision by financial regulators. Fourthly, the underlying data of the AI systems, such as client and transaction data, should be accurate, integrated, timely and consistent, and lawful regarding data sources and processing behaviors.

In 2019, the US government issued the National Artificial Intelligence Research and Development Strategic Plan, establishing federal objectives and requirements for federally-funded AI research. Under the Plan, no matter with or without a government background, all the AI research funded federally is required to build a solid and trustworthy AI management system improving fairness, transparency, accountability, and variability, capable of defending the outer attacks and handling internal errors or incidents, and opened for continuous optimization over the long term.

In the same year, the UK government proposed to place ethics as the core principle, considering that AI is encouraged on the condition that it could benefit humanity. In 2019, the European Commission issued the Ethics Guidelines for Trustworthy AI, aiming at a trustworthy AI system. These Guidelines require AI to be[4]:

- Lawful, respecting all applicable laws and regulations
- Ethical, respecting ethical principles and values
- Robust, both from a technical perspective while taking into account its social environment.

[4] European Commission (2019).

In the same year, the OECD issued the Recommendation on Artificial Intelligence (AI), putting forward five values-based principles on AI development[5]:

- Inclusive growth, sustainable development, and well-being;
- Human-centered values and fairness
- Transparency and explainability
- Robustness, security, and safety
- Accountability.

In 2017, the State Council of the People's Republic of China, upon realizing the uncertainties of the future of AI, and the challenges and risks brought by AI to the existing employment structure, laws and regulations, social ethics and values, personal privacy, and international relations, issued the Development Plan for the New Generation of AI where the Chinese government, specifies that the security risks and problems should be fully and constantly aware while encouraging and regulating the AI technology. Besides, prospective prevention measures, regulatory guidelines, and appropriate constraints should be imposed to minimize the potential risks and challenges hidden in the AI landscapes, by which a safe, reliable, and controllable AI ecosystem could be provided for the public.[6]

For the time being, AI is trudging on its road to maturity. However, doubtlessly, AI's broader and deeper application in the financial industry would encounter various obstacles regarding data, cost, security, talent, etc. Moreover, sometimes AI could cause severe problems for financial regulators and the public. For example, algorithm black box, algorithm resonance, algorithm discrimination, data dependency, and AI abuse might blur the responsibility boundaries and lead to market herd effect, financial exclusion, and privacy leakage.

While producing a positive impact on financial institutions by automating their work processes on a large scale, AI could also increase the likelihood and expand the influence of operational risk, prudential risk, reputational risk, etc. Therefore, the financial industry should, based on a combination of the general principles for AI and the characteristics of the financial industry, pay more attention to such aspects as financial security, risk controllability, subject accountability, technology comprehensibility, data security, and privacy protection (Monetary Authority of Singapore 2018).

[5] OECD council recommendation on artificial intelligence (2019).

[6] State Council of the People's Republic of China (Jul 2017) Development Plan for the New Generation of AI.

1.4 Blockchain in the Finance Sector

1.4.1 What is Blockchain?

The term "Blockchain" was brought up for the first time in 2008 by Satoshi Nakamoto in his monograph—Bitcoin: A Peer-to-peer Electronic Cash System, where he referred to the Blockchain as the most fundamental technology to construct the data structure and transaction information encryption transmission for Bitcoin, on which the mining function and transaction function of Bitcoin is built.

Nakamoto believed Blockchain technology could address the following problems in the traditional transaction model. First, in a general traditional transaction model, a third party must be involved in the supervision. Otherwise, transaction fraud cannot be avoided entirely due to a lack of trust among peers. Second, introducing a third party would increase the transaction cost and limit the feasible minimum transaction size. Third, the digital signature used in the traditional model has no electronic currency identification function; therefore, a third party is required for additional identification. To address the forgoing issues, Nakamoto created Bitcoin based on Blockchain technology.

Blockchain is a shared and immutable ledger that could facilitate the transaction recording process and assets tracking process on a business network. Assets can be classified into tangible assets (e.g., house, car, cash, and land) and intangible assets (e.g., patents, copyrights, and trademark right). Theoretically, anything of value can be tracked and traded on a Blockchain network, reducing risk and cutting costs for all involved. Blockchain is ideal for delivering information because it can provide immediate, shared, and transparent information storage with an immutable ledger to which only network members with prior permission can access. The Blockchain network can track orders, payments, accounts, production, etc. The participating members could see various transaction details from end to end.

In practice, there are three types of Blockchain technologies. They are Public Blockchain, Private Blockchain, and Consortium Blockchain, which differ in technical structure and usage. The following three paragraphs will discuss them in detail one by one.

Public Blockchain is open to various participants. Bitcoin is a typical application. Public Blockchain, following a different path from traditional centralized or quasi-centralized trust solutions, maintains its ability to ensure transaction security by the digital cryptographic model adopting the workload/equity proof mechanism. In most cases, the Public Chain is decentralized. However, there are some drawbacks of the Public Blockchain to our observations. Specifically, the Public Blockchain requires substantial computational power to operate, and it might not ensure complete confidentiality and security of the transactions based on it.

A private Blockchain network is a decentralized peer-to-peer network and therefore has no substantial difference from other distributed storage schemes in this respect. However, the most prominent feature of the Private Blockchain is that its network is governed by a unique organization whose principal functions are to control the participants allowed to enter the network, execute a consensus protocol, and maintain the shared ledger. In such a model, trust is built among limited participants on the network.

Consortium Blockchain refers to several pre-selected organizations responsible for maintaining the Blockchain on which they may submit transactions and access relevant data. The Consortium Blockchain is ideal for our transactions, as its participants should be permitted and undertake a shared responsibility for maintaining Blockchain operation.

1.4.2 Major Features of Blockchain

1.4.2.1 Distributed and Decentralized

The distributed bookkeeping technology underlying the Blockchain is constructed based on the concept of "sharing." Distributed bookkeeping allows nodes on the Blockchain to be equal to each other, and all transactions are carried out according to pre-established rules. Under distributed bookkeeping, there is no need for a third party to be involved in managing, arbitrating, or providing trust for transactions. Furthermore, any change of a node or nodes would not affect the regular operation of the Blockchain in transaction support.

Transaction information would not be stored on specific servers or the central node but shared among all nodes. Where there is a transaction, any node on the chains could be a temporary center, realizing direct peer-to-peer transactions among all nodes of the whole network.

Above all, Blockchain is distributed and decentralized, providing convenient transactions and lowering costs. It could mitigate information asymmetry and security risks in the centralized mode.[7]

1.4.2.2 Operating Under Consensus Mechanism

The Consensus Mechanism could prevent the information on the Blockchain from tampering by setting up a series of public and private keys where every node can verify the integrity and reliability of the ledger. Under the Consensus Mechanism, transaction information cannot be tampered with randomly, staying correct, truthful, and effective. In addition, information consistency is ensured among transactions whose data is stored on the books.

---

[7] The "center" (or intermediary) exists as a critical node, making it a necessary condition for traders to complete the transaction and grasp the credit status and transaction information. Traders are authorized to decide the resource price. The "center" performs the resource redistribution function and can cut off the circulation of information and resources among traders.

Every node on the Blockchain holds a copy of the complete transaction information. Even if some nodes are maliciously tampered with, other nodes would, based on the Consensus Mechanism, promptly discover the inconsistency between nodes and make adjustments in time. Therefore, any modification to the information requires the modifier to control a majority of the calculating power of the whole network. The cost would be extremely high, especially with the enormous data volume and participants.

1.4.2.3 Real-Time and Multi-node Recording

Real-time and multi-node recording provide transparency and data security for transactions. Blockchain is an open bookkeeping technology where each node synchronizes real-time transaction data, and traders are authorized to access the conditions of any node. In terms of information security, Blockchain protects participants from information stealing. During a transaction, Blockchain allows traders to access the necessary information and hides information as ordered so that traders will not be disturbed by irrelevant information while engaging in transactions.

Although Blockchain technology has become stable regarding its functionality and technical architecture, it still needs to grow. While Blockchain-related technologies such as databases, P2P networks, and cryptographic algorithms are relatively mature in processing efficiency, Blockchain still needs to adapt to environments with high-frequency processing requirements. In other words, it is reluctant to meet the needs of commercial computing for frequent and complex deals. In addition, storage capacity and expansibility of the booking and consensus mechanism should be improved.

However, Blockchain also brings big troubles to financial regulators while facilitating transactions. Issues such as data security, privacy protection, interoperability, and expansibility of on-chain storage, etc., are bothering the financial regulators in China. If these issues cannot be effectively treated by regulation, Blockchain may not be more favorable than traditional solutions, with financial regulation goals considered. According to Gartner's maturity curves of emerging technologies described in Sect. 1.1, distributed ledger technology will mature in two years after 2019, consensus mechanism and smart contracts will mature in two to five years, and zero-knowledge proof and Blockchain interoperability will mature in five to ten years.

1.4.3 Blockchain Application in the Financial Sector

In China, Blockchain is expected to have a promising future in its application in the financial sector. Above, we have introduced the key features of Blockchain in detail. The features above allow Blockchain to actively advance the number of financial businesses represented by supply chain finance, trade finance, payment and settlement, digital bills, insurance underwriting claims, and asset-backed securitization.

Traditionally, such financial businesses are multi-party scenarios lacking trust basis, which Blockchain can make up. By providing trust, Blockchain can improve the efficiency of financial resource allocation and reduce transaction costs, as proved above.

As of the end of 2022, Blockchain technology has been applied broadly and successfully in the following financial businesses in China.

1.4.3.1 Supply Chain Finance

The supply chain finance business has complex scenarios needing trust and information sharing. For example, in the supply finance business, massive subjects/participants and quantities of transaction links need mutual trust and frequent information sharing to ensure the efficiency and security of a series of transactions and procedures.

Technically, data/information on the chain is traceable, transparent, and extremely difficult to tamper. That is why Blockchain is broadly used in evidence preservation, auxiliary voucher split and circulation, smart contract automatic execution, etc. Thanks to the advantages mentioned above of Blockchain, some pain points of traditional supply chain finance businesses have been addressed. Blockchain has established the multi-level penetration of core enterprise credit and reduced the risk of manual operation.

Financial institutions worldwide have been developing and deploying Blockchain technologies in their trade finance business in recent years. For example, Barclays Bank and HSBC are exploring applying Blockchain in the letters of credit business. In addition, IBM is constructing a Blockchain trade finance platform by cooperating with various foreign banks.

In September 2018, the People's Bank of China developed a trade financial Blockchain platform, a successful first attempt to apply Blockchain technology to facilitate and support supply chain finance businesses. The platform is built based on Blockchain, which prints the supply chain finance business in transparency, credibility, security, standardization, compliance, efficiency, and public well-being. It is a shared platform capable of providing a one-station service covering registration, deposit, and the transfer of financial assets. The platform has three primary functions:

- Multi-level financing of accounts receivable
- Tax filing form for external payment
- Supervision over international trade accounts.

The three functions help the platform positively serve small and medium-sized enterprises and the real economy. By the platform, where the information is complete and valid, it would take less than 20 min from the time a client submits the loan application to the time the bank completes the deal, shortening the financing period for the clients, improving the financing efficiency and reducing the financing cost for small and medium-sized enterprises.

This example explains how Blockchain can facilitate the supply chain finance business.

1.4.3.2 Payment and Settlement

Theoretically, Blockchain payments are made directly to both parties of the transaction without any intermediaries. Therefore, if a set of distributed inter-bank financial transaction protocols is built based on Blockchain and users are provided with real-time payment and clearing services of cross-border and arbitrary currency, cross-border payment would become more convenient and less costly.

At present, major banks and financial groups worldwide have developed standards for interactive settlement by joining the R3 Blockchain Alliance. Moreover, large companies like IBM have launched cross-border payment services based on Blockchain. Besides, some Blockchain start-ups are preparing to propose new settlement standards.

1.4.3.3 Digital Bill

Digital bill is an innovation combining Blockchain and traditional bill business attributes, totally different from the conventional electronic bill system concerning their technical architectures. As a result, digital bill taking advantage of Blockchain is safer, more intelligent, more convenient, and more promising compared with the traditional electronic form.

1.4.4 Concerns Around Blockchain

1.4.4.1 Technical Concern

The good news is that Blockchain improves the security and credibility of transactions through quantities of data collection and complex consensus algorithms. The bad news is, with workload and data volume increasing, the burden on participating nodes that undertake information storage and synchronization function aggravates, which leads to a decline in system performance and operational efficiency in the existing technology environment.

For example, for the application of Blockchain in the supply chain finance business, most Blockchain services are for evidence preservation, auxiliary voucher split and circulation, smart contract automatic execution, etc., lacking a function to verify the authenticity of the on-chain information. As such, asset verification still needs manual intervention/participation.

In particular, since the financial supply chain business involves multiple subjects and links, where there is a dispute, it is tough to conduct evidence preservation and verification. Moreover, the chain protocol technology needs to be more mature for now, so there is no unified standard among the chains. As such, Blockchain at the current stage is reluctant to provide wide-fields, high-frequency and complex connections, and cross-chain interaction services.

1.4.4.2 Business Concern

Most enterprises in China have already built their chains. Those with excellent technology development or sufficient financial resources are powerful in platform construction and maintenance. Competition between chains among enterprises begins, where enterprises set quantities of data barriers, leading to information islands.

For regulators, excessive competition in Blockchain harms the financial market. The lack of information sharing or exchange among massive financial institutions will lead to a huge waste of financial resources and cause inefficiency due to the duplication of similar projects and exclusive information ownership. Therefore, to address such problems, financial regulators should play a coordinative role concerning the Blockchain development of financial institutions. More importantly, guide them to share their good practices of Blockchain to some extent, by, for example, building a semi-official sharing platform.

1.4.4.3 Regulatory Concern

For now, Chinese laws and regulations still need to clearly define the legal status and legal consequences of assets and smart contracts on the Blockchain, making it hard for traders to claim legal relief in case of any disputes.

Furthermore, distributed systems improve the difficulty of identifying the responsible subjects in case of any disputes. Most Blockchain systems are highly autonomous and data-encrypted, so the probability of illegal financial business will rise without the necessary authority (Monetary Authority of Singapore 2020).

1.5 Cloud Computing in the Financial Sector

1.5.1 What is Cloud Computing?

"Cloud" is a metaphor for the network and the Internet. Cloud used to represent the telecommunications network before. Nowadays, it is more frequently used to represent the abstraction of the Internet and its underlying infrastructures.

In China, the National Institute of Standards and Technology (the "NIST") defines Cloud Computing as a model that provides convenient and demand-oriented network access for accessing configurable computing resources sharing a pool, a platform with quantities of Internet resources including network, servers, storage, applications, and services, and users may access or acquire with minor efforts by themselves or by interacting with the service provider (Peter and Timothy 2011).

Cloud Computing has calculation power of up to 10 trillion per second, making it capable of simulating nuclear explosions and predicting climate change and market trends.

1.5.2 Features of Cloud Computing

1.5.2.1 Demand-Oriented

Cloud Computing can help financial institutions provide tailored financial services depending on the needs of their clients or customers. Besides, under Could Computing, channels of financial products and services, such as APPs, client databases, and supporting information infrastructures, can automatically adapt to fit customer habits without manual interventions by system administrators.

1.5.2.2 Extensive Access

Could Computing service can be accessed by its users through the Internet wherever and whenever. In addition, Cloud Computing supports access by various terminal devices, including but not limited to PC, laptops, and smartphones, providing great convenience for users in this Internet era in which networks and smartphones popularize.

1.5.2.3 Resources Sharing

A shared resource pool stores and manages the computing resources uploaded automatically or manually by Cloud Computing service providers. In the shared resource pool, resources placement and management, and the policies or rules thereof, are transparent, shareable, and available to various users with the help of virtualization technology.

The resources mentioned above include storage devices, data therein, and network bandwidth.

1.5.2.4 Flexible

The scale of the Cloud Computing service can automatically adapt swiftly to the changes in the business condition and workload. As such, the resources for the user are in line with their business scale, ensuring sufficient resources supply when the scale increases and avoiding resource waste when the scale decreases.

1.5.2.5 Charge Automatically

Cloud Computing allows for charging without manual intervention. The cloud system can, in compliance with laws and regulations and, as agreed by the client about privacy protection, automatically monitor the consumption records and volume of the client and accordingly calculate the amount that should charge to the client.

Based on the above five features, Cloud Computing allows users to store their personal e-mails, photos, profiles, and other information. In addition, it allows them to purchase music from service providers, find out driving and walking routes, develop websites, and interact with other users on social networking websites, through the Cloud Computing Platform.

In summary, Cloud Computing is closely related to our daily affairs. Therefore, it can improve our life and work experience by helping its users handle affairs regarding life, work, and other aspects in a swifter and more convenient way.

1.5.3 Cloud Computing Application in the Financial Sector

To begin with, we need to know about the "Financial Cloud" concept. What is Financial Cloud? What are the relations between Cloud Computing and the financial industry? In short words, Financial Cloud refers to the Cloud Computing service customized for financial institutions, including banks, securities companies, insurance companies, trust companies, FMCs (Fund Management Companies), financial leasing companies, and Internet finance platforms.

Financial Cloud, under computing and servicing functions of Cloud Computing, brings financial, customer, process, services, and value data into the "cloud" through the data center, client platform, etc. Through the cloud integration described above, Financial Cloud improves relevant systems' user experience and computing ability. In addition, it restructures data value, providing customers with better financial service experiences and, meanwhile, achieving cost reduction with regard to operation, business development, client onboarding, etc.

Financial Cloud has the following advantages.

1.5.3.1 Reduce Cost Related to IT

Financial Cloud can reduce IT-related costs of financial institutions effectively. Cloud Computing allows financial institutions to, under virtualization technology, turn physical IT devices into virtual resource pools to satisfy financial institutions' needs regarding computing power and storage. As a result, by Financial Cloud, the use efficiency of the unit IT equipment can be effectively improved, and the unit information cost reduced. That being said, the Cloud Computing architecture, compared with the traditional model relying on mainframe and microcomputer infrastructures, is far more cost-effective.

1.5.3.2 Reliable and Scalable

The traditional financial architecture emphasizes more on stability, resulting in a relatively poor expansion capacity. Therefore, under the traditional architecture, financial information systems can only be extended vertically and cannot achieve more flexible horizontal expansion. On the other hand, Cloud Computing can guarantee the reliability of financial enterprise services by multi-copy data default tolerance and interchangeable computing nodes.

Furthermore, Cloud Computing can support the performance improvements of IT systems since it adds IT devices to services and storage, where it can react simultaneously to the needs of financial institutions concerning the rapid increase or explosion of the business scale.

1.5.3.3 Higher Level of Automation

Cloud Computing can promote the automation level of operation and maintenance. For example, the Mainstream Cloud Computing Operating System, equipped with monitoring modules to manage servers, storage, and network devices of financial institutions as a unified platform, significantly improves the management capacity of their IT devices, facilitating their management of various business models with higher automation.

1.5.3.4 Managing Information Systems

Last but not least, Financial Cloud can help financial institutions by providing a unified platform to carry out or manage all their internal information systems. As a result, the information islands within the financial institutions can be mitigated and reduced, and all their internal data would be under centralized management.

Since the international financial crisis in 2008, Cloud Computing has been widely used in the financial sector. Faced with more frequent changes in the economic environment and global market than ever before, as well as the pressure from emerging e-commerce companies and FinTech companies, traditional financial institutions have no choice but to explore innovative technologies to innovate and improve their financial products and services.

Since then, numerous financial institutions worldwide have been making exploration, developing, and deployment on Cloud Computing, business optimization, and corporate strategy adjustment. In the financial sector, the supercomputing power provided by Cloud Computing and the various cloud service resources is broadly used by companies, including but not limited to financial institutions, to save their hardware resources and their IT personnel costs. In addition, while outsourcing their high-cost, non-core peripheral systems or homogeneous fundamental financial services, such entities can focus more on business and technology innovation and operation management of their core financial businesses.

1.6 Big Data in the Financial Sector

1.6.1 What is Big Data?

Regarding the definition of Big Data, each expert or research institute may give different answers. For example, Gartner, an internationally renowned information technology research institute, defined Big Data as massive information assets demanding innovative processing forms to enhance decision-making, business insights, or process optimization.

As provided by McKinsey Global Institute, Big Data is the processing of massive data on a large scale, with diverse types, constant flow, and low-value density, significantly surpassing traditional database software tools in data collection, storage, and data management and analysis.

In August 2015, the State Council of the People's Republic of China released the Notice of the State Council on Issuing the Action Outline for Promoting the Development of Big Data, defining Big Data as data sets characterized by high volume, more varieties, high velocity, and high application value, and is rapidly developing into a new generation of information technology and service type for collection, storage, and correlation analysis of vast amounts of data from disparate sources and in various forms whereby a human can discover new knowledge, create new value, and improve the capabilities.

Technically, the relationship between Big Data and Cloud Computing is like the opposite side of a coin. The generation and development of Big Data technology require massive data with large sample sizes and consume more IT resources. The application of Cloud Computing has solved the performance bottleneck problem of dealing with massive data.

1.6.2 Features of Big Data

1.6.2.1 Not Necessary to Be "Big"

Big Data does not have to be "Big," i.e., massive. "Small" data generated by traditional information systems is also essential to Big Data analysis. The underlying data and data sets of Big Data mainly concentrate on the Internet, the Internet of Things, and traditional information systems, among which the Internet of Things occupies the most significant proportion.

1.6.2.2 Complex Analysis Structure

Big Data consists of structured, unstructured, and semi-structured data, posing a great challenge and an opportunity to the traditional data analysis method. It is the reason for the origin and development of Big Data technology.

1.6.2.3 Low Data Value Density

Compared with traditional information systems, Big Data has low data value density and, therefore, can complete the data value extraction process faster and more conveniently, which is the core competitiveness of Big Data platforms.

1.6.2.4 Expand Very Fast

In the past, the data increment of traditional information systems was predictable and controllable. However, in the Big Data era, the data growth rate is far beyond that of traditional data, and the processing capacity has exceeded its limit. Data growth is a relative concept.

1.6.3 Big Data Application in the Financial Sector

Big Data finance refers to using Big Data technology to process massive data through the Internet, Cloud Computing, etc., to carry out innovative financial services combined with traditional financial business. Although traditional financial institutions have deposited many payment flow data, much Big Data still needs to be fully and effectively utilized due to the business segmentation of various departments.

For now, more and more Internet enterprises have become the leaders in Big Data financial business based on their technology and user resources. Faced with it, traditional financial institutions strengthen internal data integration, using Big Data technology to expand the business and carry out personalized financial services. Based on the in-depth analysis and mining of Big Data, financial institutions can have a better understanding of customers, clearly understand the life stage and wealth stage of customers, change from simply capturing customers' financial behavior to capturing social behavior and life behavior, and grasp the complete customer data, to draw the financial portrait of customer dynamics.

Meanwhile, by applying the AI cognitive model, users, including but not limited to financial institutions, upon accelerating the multi-angle customer classification, rather than be confined to the existing group classification standards, can cluster customers with high granularity and create unprecedented customer segmentations, by which, they develop and deploy accurate product penetration scheme, financial asset allocation scheme, and value-added services personalized scheme, etc., to provide differentiated as well as comprehensive financial services (Wang and Zhou 2019).

There are two models in this respect.

1.6.3.1 Platform Finance Model

In the platform financial model, platforms use their own Big Data to conduct professional data mining through the Internet, Cloud Computing, and other information processing methods. Then, they combine it with traditional financial services to provide enterprises with services such as financing and settlement. This model relies on the trading platform and the data generated in the transaction process, which is the foundation for the platform to mine customer needs, analyze and understand customers, and provide financial services for customers.

Finance deals with risk, and credit evaluation is the core of risk control. In the platform finance model, the platform can quickly conduct credit evaluations and provide credit services by mining transaction data. Moreover, credit evaluation based on Big Data can produce more accurate outcomes than traditional methods. As a result, it can effectively solve the problem of risk control and reduce the rate of bad accounts.

1.6.3.2 Supply Chain Finance Model

In this model, the core enterprises in the supply chain can depend on their business advantages to provide financial services to the upstream and downstream partners by controlling the Big Data on cash flow, orders, purchase, and sales flow, using their funds, or cooperating with financial institutions. The supply chain finance model originated in the Netherlands in the nineteenth century and gradually matured by the late twentieth century, which originated from the fact that in a complete supply chain, the capital situation of enterprises at each node is uneven, and the lack of capital at a particular node may affect the efficiency of the whole supply chain. With a robust core enterprise, all participants in the entire supply chain can be provided with enough financial support and service to meet the collaborative industrial chain development goal. However, traditional supply chain finance only aims at the industrial chain of a specific industry. In contrast, modern supply chain finance, relying on the Internet and Big Data technology, can cover a broader range.

Jingdong has mastered massive transaction data of related enterprises of various categories, industries, and regions, providing a basis for it to evaluate enterprise credit and fund utilization through data mining, providing help in the cases of using future earnings as a guarantee, obtaining bank credit, and providing financial support and services for suppliers. In the supply chain finance model, Jingdong implements two-way binding with banks and suppliers, where suppliers must cooperate with Jingdong for a long time to enjoy the services of long-term payment, logistics, credit services, and loans provided by Jingdong. The banking sector will also have to rely on the Big Data of Jingdong to achieve rapid and accurate credit evaluation for their clients. Through cooperation with suppliers and banks, Jingdong has integrated logistics, information flow, and capital flow to achieve a win–win situation.

1.7 Retrospect and Prospect of China's FinTech Market

As of 2021, China's FinTech market is one of the largest in the world, with a total transaction value of over USD 29 trillion. This market includes various financial services, such as mobile payments, online lending, and digital wealth management. The growth of FinTech in China has been driven by factors such as high Internet and mobile phone penetration, a large and growing middle class, and government support for innovation in financial services. According to a report by Statista, the total transaction value in China's FinTech market was expected to grow with a projected annual rate of 11.9% between 2021 and 2025.

China's mobile payment market is dominated by two major players: Alipay and WeChat Pay. According to a report by iResearch, in 2020, the total transaction value of China's mobile payment market reached RMB 59.8 trillion (USD 9.3 trillion), with Alipay and WeChat Pay accounting for 55.1% and 38.8% of the market share, respectively. In addition, China's online lending market has also experienced rapid growth in recent years. According to a report by iResearch, the transaction size of China's online lending market reached RMB 3.95 trillion (USD 614.3 billion) in 2020, with a year-on-year growth rate of 9.2%.

China has been a leader in adopting Blockchain technology, AI, Big Data, and Cloud Computing in its FinTech industry, with many companies and start-ups exploring the potential of these technologies to disrupt traditional financial services.

Blockchain technology has been widely adopted in China's FinTech industry, particularly in digital currencies and supply chain finance. In 2014, the PBOC established a research group to study the potential use of Blockchain technology in financial applications. Since then, China has become a global leader in Blockchain development, with many start-ups and established companies exploring the potential of this technology. According to a report by Blockdata, as of August 2021, there were 6,063 Blockchain-related companies in China, with a total investment of USD 10.8 billion.

AI and Big Data are also being used extensively in China's FinTech industry, particularly in risk management, fraud detection, and credit scoring. Concerning AI, Many companies use machine learning and natural language processing to analyze data and make predictions about market trends and consumer behavior. China's big tech companies, such as Alibaba, Tencent, and Baidu, have been investing heavily in AI, and many FinTech start-ups are also exploring the potential of AI to improve their services. About Big Data, companies can gain insights into customer behavior and preferences to improve their products and services by analyzing large amounts of data. For example, Zhima Credit, an Alibaba subsidiary, uses AI and Big Data to provide credit scores and risk assessments for individuals and small businesses. The platform processes over 3,000 data points from various sources, including social media, shopping history, and financial transactions, to generate credit scores.

Cloud Computing is also widely adopted in China's FinTech industry, allowing companies to store and process large amounts of data quickly and efficiently. Cloud Computing also enables companies to scale their operations quickly and easily without investing in expensive infrastructure. For example, WeBank, China's first digital-only bank, uses Cloud Computing to provide its customers with various financial services, including loans, wealth management, and insurance.

As such, adopting these technologies in China's FinTech industry has brought significant benefits, including increased efficiency, improved customer experience, and reduced costs. As a result, these technologies are expected to continue to play a vital role in the growth and development of China's FinTech industry. Overall, China's FinTech industry is well-positioned to take advantage of these technologies, and we can expect continued innovation and disruption in the years to come (Yu 2018).

References

Andy H, Chief Economist, Bank of England, Speech at the Maxwell Fry Annual Global Finance Lecture (29 Oct 2014) Managing global finance as a system. Birmingham University, p 10

China Institute of Information and Communications Research (Jan 2018) Research on the development trend and application scenarios of China's financial technology frontier technology. https://www.sohu.com/a/217117842_735021

Du M (2018) Mobile payment recognition technology based on face detection algorithm. Concurr Comput Pract Exp 30

European Commission (Apr 2019) Ethics guidelines for trustworthy AI

Huang Y, Huang Z (2018) China's digital finance development: present and future. Econ. Q. (17)

Lin Z (2017) Opportunities, risks and prevention and control strategies of artificial intelligence payment. Financ Technol Era (25)

Liu X (2017) Credit investigation AI: credit service from artificial intelligence. Contemporary Financier, no 12

Lu L, Yao Y (2015) New financial era. CITIC Press

Mo F, Zhao D (2017) Technology reshapes financial: fintech practice and outlook. China Finance Press

Monetary Authority of Singapore (Nov 2018) Principles to promote fairness, ethics, accountability and transparency (FEAT) in the use of artificial intelligence and data analytics in Singapore's financial sector

Monetary Authority of Singapore (Feb 2020) Cyber risk surveillance: a case study of Singapore. MAS stuff paper, no 57

OECD, Council Recommendation on AI (May 2019). https://legalinstruments.oecd.org/en/instruments/OECD-LEGAL-0449

Peter M, Timothy G (28 Sep 2011) The NIST definition of cloud computing-recommendations of the national institute of standards and technology. NIST Special Publication 800-145

Wang B, Zhou Y (2019) From digital to data: research on digital transformation of credit reporting system. Credit Reporting, no 08

Yu F (2018) FinTech: big data, blockchain and artificial intelligence applications and future. Zhejiang University Press

Chapter 2
FinTech is Impacting the Financial Industry

Introduction

FinTech is impacting traditional financial businesses. Traditional financial institutions are innovating their business models by applying FinTech, represented by AI, Blockchain, Cloud Computing, and Big Data, for business model optimization. As a result, they simplify their business processes, improve their business efficiency, reduce costs, and increase their profits.

Furthermore, with the advent of the FinTech economy, a number of FinTech business models, FinTech products, and FinTech services are emerging in the financial market, profoundly affecting the supply mode of financial services and injecting innovative vitality into the financial industry.

2.1 FinTech in the Banking Industry

2.1.1 FinTech Benefits Commercial Banks

Banking is a technology-intensive industry closely related to scientific and technological innovation regarding its development. In recent years, FinTech has innovated financial products, service models, and customer acquisition channels for various commercial banks and accordingly impacts the business model and profits of the banking industry (Xie et al. 2018).

Provided that other investment factors remain unchanged and the original business model and organizational management structure are maintained, FinTech can promote emerging market development, exhibition mode innovation, and cost-saving regarding internal and external communication and coordination among banks. Moreover, it can also directly improve their overall performance and business efficiency.

D. Zhao et al., *FinTech and SupTech in China*, Contributions to Finance and Accounting,
https://doi.org/10.1007/978-981-99-5173-4_2

Commercial banks, while their business model and efficiency in communication and coordination are improved by their investment in FinTech, described above, adjust and reform their organizational structure, human capital management, and business process. During this process, various producing elements interact collaboratively, further promoting the operating performance of financial institutions and providing an indirect productivity return on FinTech investment by them (Jin et al. 2020).

In August 2019, the People's Bank of China released the FinTech Development Plan (2019–2021), which provides that, among others, FinTech has the following advantages:

- Streamline the links of transactions between the providers (i.e., commercial banks) and their customers
- Reduce the marginal cost of financing business
- Open up new ways/methods to reach/interact with customers
- Promote the sustained optimization of financial institutions about their profit models, business forms, assets and liabilities, lender-borrower relationship, and conduit expansion.

By actively utilizing such advantages, the banks are enhancing their core competitiveness in the process of FinTech transformation facing massive institutions. Ultimately, the banking industry's upgrading is realized with various banks' efforts.

FinTech is impacting the banking industry in various aspects. This book lists hereunder some typical examples for your better understanding.

2.1.1.1 Big Data Changes the Business Attitude of Banks

With the advent and popularity of digitalization, banks have collected a large amount of customer data through their various businesses, stored on their Internet platforms or in their internal database. To better design financial products to meet customers' needs, they need to deploy Big Data analysis for in-depth mining, understanding customer needs, categorizing customer types, and improving their customer service level.

With Big Data technology, banks can change their traditional risk control measures, such as offline audits, mortgage guarantee, etc. In addition, they can directly integrate massive data to form their users' portraits and formulate personalized pricing, which helps them, for example, speed up their lending process.

What is more, Big Data analysis is also helpful for the banks to accurately evaluate the business development trend to make on-time intervention measures to seek advantages and avoid disadvantages, enhance profitability, and achieve benign development of the business. Furthermore, in risk monitoring, banks can use Big Data to build an internal risk monitoring mechanism to monitor credit transactions, reduce the probability of financial fraud, and prevent credit incidents.

2.1.1.2 Blockchain Optimizes the Business Processes of Banks

As introduced in Chap. 1, Blockchain has significant features, including decentralized and de-trust. These features allow Blockchain to simplify the intermediate links of real-time transactions and shorten the working processes of the banks.

In addition, Blockchain can be widely applied in cross-border payment and settlement, digital bills, and credit since it can technically build a set of large-scale and low-cost information networks, providing technical support in creating innovative business models and reducing potential expenditure.

2.1.1.3 Cloud Computing Promotes Resource Integration and Optimization

Technically, the Cloud Computing platform allows the banks to integrate and sort out all kinds of information resources for data sharing, data management, and unified scheduling. In addition, some banks may lease their information resources and their ERP systems, through their cloud platforms, to other financial institutions which, are therefore legally authorized, in compliance with applicable laws, regulations, and contracts, to obtain detailed financial data and information of their clients and accordingly evaluate the credit risks of them.

2.1.1.4 AI Improves the Quality of Financial Products and Services

With the technical advantages of AI, banks can have a deeper understanding of their customers. Based on such understanding, they can explore intelligent products and services to meet the personalized needs of their customers and improve the customer experience, which is vital to test the level of their service and prove their core competitiveness in the future.

AI products can be applied to facilitate various business scenarios of banks. For example, intelligent recognition can be applied by banks to identify customers. Furthermore, intelligent robots can be applied to respond to customers promptly and substitute manual efforts regarding simple or highly repetitive tasks, such as inquiries or card applications. From this, the banks improve their work efficiency through the Robot Process Automation (RPA) method.

2.1.2 FinTech is Impacting the Competitive Pattern Among Banks

In the traditional sense, the outlets of the banks serve as the major channel and window for their business. The volume of the outlets directly determines their capacity for customer acquisition, maintenance, facility limits, financial services, customer marketing, business consulting, and cultural display. In summary, the outlet is the basis for the banks to enlarge their business scale and market share and improve their competitiveness.

However, with FinTech broadly applied in the banking sector, the role played by traditional outlets for the banks is constantly weakening. Under this irreversible trend, banks are exploring transforming traditional outlets to make them more convenient, intelligent, and integrated.

In actuality, the impact of FinTech on the outlets is only a microcosm of its impact on the competition pattern among banks. Nevertheless, till now, there have long been arguments over the impact of FinTech on the competition mode of the banking sector.

According to Hauswald and Marquez (2003), Information Technology has a dual effect on the competition mode within banks. On the one hand, Information Technology improves banks' capacity to process information and data. As a result, certain banks with more outstanding technical and financial resources take more market power and monopolize the market. On the other hand, under Information Technology, massive data is to be disseminated and shared within the whole industry, creating a fairer market environment, mitigating the monopoly problem, and promoting market competition (Hauswald and Marquez 2003).

According to the World Bank (2016), digital technology also has a dual effect on industrial competition. On the one hand, digital technology boosts economies and forms a natural monopoly by reducing the marginal cost of certain banks, but not all, which harms the market competition; on the other hand, digital technology can remove market entry barriers and promote market competition (World Bank 2016).

From the above two cases with similar attributes and backgrounds, FinTech, as a further development thereof, also has a dual effect on the competition in the banking sector. On the one hand, with tech giants entering the banking sector, the competition therein will become fiercer, and the living environment for banks will become more severe. On the other hand, while the Internet and technology enterprises begin to eat the market share of the banking industry with their better customer experience and lower operating costs, traditional banks are forced to transform to counterattack or survive. This process promotes the advancement of the banking industry (Qiu et al. 2018).

2.1.3 The Advent of Open Banking Ecology

What is Open Banking? "Open Banking" refers to a new set of business and technology integration systems built following openness, sharing, and win–win. Open Banking is about, under the technical support from Internet, Information Technology, AI, etc., and driven by arousing scenarios, building an ecology system that integrates various scenarios and standardized digital interfaces connecting different industries.

In essence, Open Banking provides its users with non-inductive, seamless, and boundless financial services based on optimizing the banks' technical structures, customer interaction methods, and risk control measures. The past years have witnessed the significance of Open Banking in the global banking industry.

From our surveys, Open Banking has the following potential benefits:

- Improve the customer experience
- Create new revenue sources for the banks
- Promote the inclusiveness of financial services.

Besides, Open Banking can promote innovation and competition between banks and other market participants (i.e., non-banking financial institutions and non-financial entities). However, it might also bring about a brand new financial services ecosystem, where the traditional roles played by the banks might change significantly.

2.1.3.1 Background of Open Banking

The issue of government affairs transparency has been a hot topic among the public in the past years. The transparency of specific government data has economic value, enabling market entities to save costs by more explicit expectations and promoting market development by giving birth to new enterprises, products, and services.

For now, data has been recognized as an essential productive factor and strategic resource by many countries. That being said, the economic value of data and data sharing have been broadly recognized.

With the development of the Internet, the volume of data exposes. Under such a background, the demand for data opening and sharing gradually shifts from the government to the financial market participants. Banks hold the most proportion of financial data throughout the financial industry, whose transparency has aroused concerns in recent years.

A key technology closely related to Open Banking is Application Programming Interface (API), which can fully utilize various enterprise resources, giving birth to a new economy form—"API economy."

The API is designed to enable the users to directly access programs based on particular software or hardware without the need to access the source code or understand the details of the whole internal working mechanism. For example, service providers may provide their technical services via API on the supply side. On the demand side, service demanders may access the interface through parameters. In such a model, different technologies can stick to each other based on business logic and data, fulfilling the data circulation and sharing purpose.

The API can be classified into internal API, joint API, and open API. Among them, the open API is user-centered and continuously enriches and improves the targeted application(s) with the vast third-party force to improve user engagement and coupling degree, where the API application ecology has formed gradually.

Enterprises may share their data, services, and business capabilities in the form of API with other participants in the API ecosystem, forming a brand new interconnection mode with regard to business capabilities, a brand new value network of symbiosis, and a win–win situation among various participants. The value network can organize customer-centered resources from developers, suppliers, dealers, after-sales servers, and financial institutions, forming a platform-based Internet connection model—the API economic model which allows financial institutions to capture the needs of Internet users and integrate themselves into the Internet ecology in a swifter and more flexible way.

Throughout 2020, the API has brought significant economic benefits to Internet giants. For example, in 2020,

- API contributed over 50% of the annual revenue of Salesforce
- Google processed transactions amounting to roughly 5 billion dollars per day through the API
- Twitter processed transactions amounting to roughly 13 billion dollars per day through the API
- Amazon processed transactions amounting to 100 billion dollars per day through the API.

API has significantly promoted the advent and development of Open Banking.

2.1.3.2 Open Banking from Global Perspectives

At the end of 2015, the European Union issued the Payment Service Directive 2 ("PSD2"), providing non-banking enterprises with the opportunity to compete with the banks concerning payment business and consumers with more options regarding financial products and services. In August 2017, France issued the Monetary and Financial Code (Revised), incorporating the PSD2 into France's national legislation. However, the revised code did not put substantial interventions upon Open Banking. In 2016, the first specific Open Banking policy was officially enacted by the United Kingdom—the Open Banking Standard (the "OBS").

The Competition and Markets Authority (the "CMA") conducted a survey researching the retail banking market and officially released in August 2016 a report concluding that, among others, while older and larger banks are not competitive enough in customer business, Open Banking can provide customers with additional options to compare when shopping. According to the report, Open Banking is designed to encourage innovation, transparency, and competition. In addition, it aims to provide APIs, data structures, and security architectures, enabling customers to share their financial records conveniently and securely.

Based on the survey, the CMA established the Open Banking Implementation Entity (the "OBIE") and reserved its power to determine the governance, composition, and budget. The OBIE is financially funded by the nine largest banks (the "CMA9") and is regulated collaboratively by the United Kingdom Capital Markets Authority, the Financial Conduct Authority, and the UK Treasury. In June 2020, the UK government launched the Open Banking services platform where individuals and institutions may choose the products and services they want, and third-party companies may search for the technical solutions they want. As of April 2020, 74 banks and 134 third-party service providers in the United Kingdom had joined as members of the OBIE.

Apart from the United Kingdom, many other countries or regions have also promoted specific policies to encourage Open Banking, but in different ways. In 2018, Mexico issued the FinTech Act with multiple clauses regulating Open Banking. In 2020, the Japan Financial Services Agency ("JFSA") kicked off API. The Monetary Authority of Singapore enacted the Financial Services API Guidance Manual, advocating a non-mandatory and organic transition to Open Banking. In 2018, The United States issued API standards similar to the PSD2 but not mandatory for banks. In 2019, Australia passed the Consumer Data Power Rules, requiring ANZ, Westpac, Commonwealth Bank, and National Australia to share product data with recognized recipients by data owners at request. The Consumer Data Power Rules make it legally mandatory for banks to allow customers to acquire, access, and share with third parties their data. Brazil and Hong Kong chose to provide guidance or policy framework at the regulatory level, aiming to gradually allow the users to access their financial data, including but not limited to demand deposits, savings accounts, payment accounts and credit, foreign exchange, investment, insurance, and open pension, etc. Financial regulators in India, South Korea, and Taiwan have also officially expressed their intentions to encourage Open Banking.

2.1.3.3 Reflection and Expectation to Open Banking Development

In recent years, more and more banks in Europe and the United States have adopted the Open banking model. Some large banks, such as Banco Bilbao Vizcaya Argentaria (the "BBVA"), Citi Bank, Capital One, and Barclays, prefer to open their APIs by independently constructing their platforms to match the business ecologies of various industries. In addition, some emerging banks are working with other types of financial services providers to explore the underserved market, starting from account plug-in services. On the other hand, some small and medium-sized banks with tight capital and weak technology have little intention for dependent development and may therefore develop in cooperation with others or directly borrow platforms from third parties to connect with the upper-level ecology of Open Banking in any feasible and economical methods.

In order to effectively deploy the Open Banking ecology, the banks should consider their interests and the prudent operation need, and accordingly prepare a timeline and take actions step by step. During the implementation process, the banks need to circulate data with various entities, in which other participating entities might challenge their control over data, their market dominance status, and even their profits.

Meanwhile, some problems are brothering the banks. For example, under the regulatory environment emphasizing prudent operation, data security, and privacy protection, the banks have compliance concerns over the reform of financial data sharing. Moreover, some banks are complaining that it is unfair that, under the current data-sharing model, they have to pay the cost of data activities that benefit the FinTech companies, which are their competitors.

From the industrial perspective, a mature, stable, and clear Open Banking model has yet to be formed in the global scope for the time being. Therefore, our current practices on Open Banking are merely at an initial exploration stage. However, in the future, with countries constantly releasing encouraging policies and according to the development trends of former technologies (e.g., Internet), we expect that the Open Banking ecology will be broadly recognized, adopted, and implemented around the world, and the business models therein will expand from retail business to institutional business.

2.1.4 Information Leakage and Abuse, the Most Challenge

Open Banking breaks the current interest balance among banks, FinTech companies, and their customers, and from a data processing perspective, among data controllers, data users, and owners. Europe's advance in encouraging Open Banking development responds to the implementation of the General Data Protection Regulation (the "GDPR") enacted by the European Union in 2018, regarded as the "strictest ever" data-related regulation. For Open Banking development, such issues as data sharing, data security, and privacy protection should be addressed by relevant regulations. A number of problems or incidents may occur if the corresponding regulatory environment regarding the data protection of banks stays stagnant.

2.1.4.1 Data Leakage Risk in Storage and Transmission

To some extent, the Open Banking model weakens the role of financial institutions as the "gatekeeper" of customers' information. Under the principle of data sharing, the information and data of customers are to be held and stored within a broader range of institutions and transmitted at a higher frequency among such institutions.

With increased storage locations and data transmission frequency, customer data is more likely to leak, with or without human factors, or be attacked by hackers. Whatever the causes are, data leakage will seriously impact the brands of the corresponding banks, causing reputational risks for them.

2.1.4.2 Inadequate Regulatory Standards

With the increase of data dimensions and volume under the progress of data-related technologies (e.g., machine learning), previously, the data processing and transmission standards considered secure and reliable may no longer be rational and need adjustments as appropriate. Furthermore, under insufficient regulatory standards, reverse reduction of desensitized data is more likely to occur, further increasing customer data and personal information leakage risk.

2.1.4.3 Information Asymmetry

Open Banking might exacerbate the information asymmetry between providers and their customers. Providers that are good at and benefit from data analysis like to collect a broader range of customer data, creating an omniscient and invisible "God perspective" status for them. In other words, there is an information asymmetry convenient for the providers to take advantage of the habits and vulnerabilities. As a result, they might mislead their consumers out of profiting motives or conduct fraud.

Overall, information asymmetry equips financial providers with the ability to discriminate and exclude vulnerable groups instead of promoting efficiency and innovation as expected. Self-disciplinary efforts could not address these defects due to their profiting motives and therefore need external intervention from regulators.

2.1.4.4 Cross-Jurisdiction Exacerbates Data Abuse

Although Open Banking has become a global trend, encouraging regulatory policies and institution types, differ among countries. In the future, the Open Banking model will be more conducive to the leading banks' rapid expansion regarding their international business layouts. However, as the related business and partners of those leading banks may cross jurisdictions, data abuse may be further amplified in the context of legal and regulatory differences, placing consumers in a more vulnerable position.

2.2 FinTech in the Securities Industry

Information Technology and FinTechs, including AI, Blockchain, Cloud Computing, and Big Data, have also injected new vitality into the high-quality development of the securities industry in recent years. As a result, the integration between technology and the securities business is deepening during the process. Furthermore, securities companies are changing their strategies and thoughts about the Internet, data, and intelligence.

2.2.1 FinTech is Impacting the Securities Industry

At an early stage in the securities industry, business model innovation refers to electrification and informatization. Around the world, in 1969, Autex, the world's first financial trading system, connected by telephone lines to handle block trade of institutional investors, delivered an average of 15 bulk deals a day for a total of $5.2 million. In 1971, the NASDAQ Stock Exchange was established as the world's first automatic quotation stock exchange, whose securities dealer automatic quotation system was a complete electronic trading system. The Intermarket Trading System officially emerged in the United States in 1978, connecting the New York Stock Exchange, Boston Stock Exchange, and other markets. In the middle and late 1990s, the rapid development of Internet technology made the Internet brokerage business a reality. Internet brokerages gradually replaced the traditional brokerage model driven by telephone and counter.

Since 2009, with the deepening of the integration between finance and technology, many large investment banks have begun to increase their investment in FinTech. Moreover, in December 2015, NASDAQ used Blockchain technology to complete and record private securities transactions for the first time, which is a significant milestone with regard to the application of Blockchain. Besides, other stock exchanges worldwide, such as the Australian Stock Exchange and the Japan Exchange Group, have also been promoting the proof-of-concept testing of Blockchain technology in capital market infrastructure in recent years.

Although China's securities industry started relatively late due to historical factors, it has developed rapidly in the past two decades. For FinTech, China has, in recent years, by reference to international peer experience and based on domestic conditions, carried out a number of frontier applications regarding Cloud Computing, Big Data, etc. For example, some major Chinese securities brokers have launched AI Advisor modules to analyze transaction preferences through Big Data or algorithms, providing their institutional clients with quantitative models, portfolio strategies, and asset allocation services.

China is playing a leading role in FinTech around the world, especially in digital payment. Nevertheless, the securities industry needs to catch up regarding FinTech's application and technical innovation and has to borrow foreign models in this respect. Under this background, the Chinese securities industry is trying to leverage FinTech for its digital transformation, which broadens the securities business, changes the operating model, risk control and compliance manners, and gives birth to new types of financial products and services, including AI Advisor, intelligent research, Financial Cloud, etc. This exploration, as proved by practices, effectively improves the user experience, dramatically reduces operating costs, and optimizes the operational efficiency of the market as a whole.

2.2.2 *FinTech Application in the Securities Industry*

2.2.2.1 Drive the Digitalization of Securities Companies

With the rapid development of Big Data, Cloud Computing, biometrics, neural network, and intelligent hardware, the application of FinTech in the securities industry is deepening and expanding. For the front end of the securities industry, FinTech promotes the securities business transforming from online diversion at an early stage to innovative forms represented by precision marketing, intelligent customer service, AI Advisor, etc. For the middle-end and back-end of the securities industry, FinTech is increasing its influence on the organization construction and operation mode of securities companies.

Nowadays, more and more securities companies have begun to carry out online. Intelligent businesses leverage Cloud Computing to construct resource pools equipped with functions, including computing, storage, server, and network, realizing resource sharing and automatized management within the company, by which they improve their management efficiency and expand the scope of such efficiency to more scenarios.

For example, Big Data enables securities companies to collect and leverage internal and external data more efficiently and to analyze the data sources, data characteristics, evolution trends, and potential impact, optimizing their decision-making, business operation, marketing, sales, risk control, and compliance. Furthermore, securities companies can form three-dimensional and accurate customer portraits of their clients through Big Data, giving full play to the data value and thoroughly improving their overall compliance management and risk control level.

Another example is the AI application. Securities companies may also leverage AI technologies to build cloud platforms to optimize Big Data-based algorithm trading based on Big Data, launching AI architects in various fields to provide more tailored services for customers, reduce operating costs, and increase asset allocation efficiency.

Furthermore, Blockchain could, with its features such as openness, transparency, tamper-proof, and convenience to track, provide securities companies with innovative solutions addressing the multiple challenging issues existing in the securities industry, such as data security and customer credit verification. Several securities companies in China have already initiated relevant explorations and research.

Last but not least, the utilization and application of FinTech may provide securities companies and their branches with more flexibility in their organizational structures and internal functions. While saving the workforce, FinTech requires securities to be equipped with more FinTech-specialized talents.

2.2.2.2 Improve Securities Quantitative Investment

Quantitative investment consolidates underlying data and outer compiling environment and uses computer program language to construct a financial data research system. In the overseas market, quantitative investment has been relatively mature after developing for decades and has gradually become a major investment means by global financial institutions. According to statistics, more than 80% of the large FMCs (Fund Management Companies) in the United States and a third of the large fund managers in Asia use quantitative investment strategies and quantitative means.

By definition, quantitative investment refers to an investment method utilizing quantitative methods and computer programming to trade securities instructions for obtaining stable returns. Quantitative investment tools cover the entire investment management process, including quantitative stock selection, quantitative timing, stock index futures arbitrage, commodity futures arbitrage, statistical arbitrage, algorithm trading, asset allocation, and risk control.

Compared with traditional investment methods, quantitative investment relies more on mathematical models and underlying data. As a result, decisions reached by quantitative strategies are more objective, rational, and scientific, where subjective investments can be effectively avoided. Since capital markets worldwide are becoming increasingly complex, the traditional way of making investment decisions should be challenged and reformed. Advanced transaction execution algorithms contain various complex quantitative models capable of managing market and liquidity risks in the transaction process, providing a window for the development of quantitative investment.

For now, in China, the scale of quantitative trading is small on the whole. Only a few securities and private equity investment companies have built their quantitative teams. In contrast, quantitative models and systems have been widely used in enterprise risk management.

2.2.2.3 AI Investment Advisor

AI Investment Advisor leverages Big Data analysis, quantitative financial models, and intelligent algorithms to analyze their customers' risk profile, financial status, cash flow, and investment appetite to provide diversified, automatic, personalized, and intelligent financial services to customers. AI Investment Advisor is designed to provide qualified investors identified by prescribed questionnaires with automated asset management services and investment advice meeting their risk appetite through computer and quantitative trading technology. The services above may cover stock allocation, bond allocation, stock options operation, real estate asset allocation, etc.

Compared with traditional investment advisory tools, AI Investment Advisor has advantages with regard to reducing decision-making costs, diversifying investment risks, and predicting risks (e.g., Black Swan) since it can provide higher-level systematization, intelligence, and automation with regard to data processing activities (data collection included) which, cover both front-end functions such as investment decisions and middle-end and back-end functions such as risk control and operation management. Furthermore, considering the potentiality of AI Investment Advisors, massive subjects, including but not limited to traditional financial institutions, technology companies, internet financial platforms, and PE managers, are exploring AI Investment Advisor layouts and business scenarios.

Traditional investment institutions leverage Big Data analysis and AI algorithms to improve the effectiveness and accuracy of their investment decisions, especially quantitative investment decisions. Technology companies focus more on AI Advisor design as their role in the market is to provide a network-based AI Investment Advisor platform solely to mitigate or address the information asymmetry among investors, especially individual investors. In the past, investment services by financial institutions were solely for high-end customers. With the advent of AI Investment Advisor, investment services are empowered to be price-favorable, convenient, and popular. While traditional investment advisers charge more than 1% for management, AI Investment Advisors charge only in the region of 0.3%. This favorable pricing makes AI Investment Advisor more attractive to the general public.

With respect to evolution, AI Investment Advisor originated in the United States as a general digital online investment analysis tool and underwent three development stages after that.

- Stage one: Online Investment Advisor

By the late 1990s, investment analysis tools provided for investors had been greatly improved with regard to technological advances and customers. However, machine learning had yet to come out, and investment analysis tools at that time were mainly in the online form, used for online portfolio analysis in most cases.

- Stage two: Robo Investment Advisor

The second stage started in 2008 when a large number of technology enterprises began to provide digital investment tools based on machine learning. In this period, Robo Advisor emerged and further deepened machine intelligence applications in the securities businesses. Specifically, machine learning was broadly applied in customer analysis and asset allocation in China.

- Stage three: AI Investment Advisor

With the advent and breakthrough of AI and Cloud Computing, AI Investment Advisor system was designed and developed to function, covering the whole value chain of investment management with the least manual interference. Compared with Robo Advisor, AI Advisor is constructed based on AI and Cloud Computing, breaking down the user boundaries in traditional investment advisory tools and enabling massive long-tail customers to acquire investment advisory services at low cost. According to statistics, AI Investment Advisor serves around ten million customers in China.

In the United States, in February 2017, the Securities and Exchange Commission (the "SEC") issued the Guidance Update: Robo-Advisers, where it implicitly classified AI Investment Advisor as investment advisers capable of providing plenipotentiary service for investors and required licensed operating and regulation from the Investment Advisor Act of 1940.

In China, the AI Investment Advisor market is still immature. For now, many financial institutions have developed and deployed Robo Investment Advisors rather than AI investment Advisors. That being said, the role of AI investment Advisor has yet to be widely recognized by China's domestic market and therefore has vast potential.

These years have witnessed an increasingly complex international economic environment and drastic fluctuations in various asset prices, significantly increasing the demand for professional wealth management. Meanwhile, the wealth management industry is undergoing a series of transformations, from extensive style to refined and professional style, from household management orientation to institutional management orientation. Against this background, FinTech can solve the pain points during the transformations since it can effectively meet customers' diversified wealth management needs by providing customized and tailored wealth management services, where the intelligent wealth management mode is formed gradually becoming a trend.

Also, the COVID-19 epidemic has significantly increased Chinese individuals' and families' willingness to invest online. As a result, after these three years, online investment and online assets management have become more acceptable to Chinese people, accelerating the online business transformation progress by wealth management companies.

Under the development and inter-function of the real economy and the financial industry, financial products in the securities market are increasingly enriched. Also, under the continuous efforts on financial education by Chinese financial regulators, Chinese citizens' knowledge of asset management has improved and become more mature. This trend injects greater vitality into China's wealth management industry from the demand side.

2.3 FinTech in the Insurance Industry

2.3.1 FinTech is Impacting the Insurance Industry

In the past few years, "Online Insurance" and "Insurance-Tech" have come to the public's eyesight, along with the technical maturity of Information Technology and its broad application in the financial sector. With respect to data in the insurance industry, FinTech can be leveraged by the insurance industry to more efficiently and effectively process relevant data for better risk control, inter governance, and outer regulation. From China's practices, FinTech impacts the insurance industry from four aspects—channel, product, technology, and concept.

2.3.1.1 Channel

The Internet channel (i.e., online mode) can break through the geographical restrictions among insurance companies, their agents, and their other business partners. In other words, the Internet allows them to deliver their products and services to customers located around the country, or even the world, regardless of the time and location limits, increasing their business volume as well as saving costs with regard to marketing, sales, distribution, and internal management, etc.

2.3.1.2 Product

FinTech can change the habits of customers. For example, Alipay has made online shopping and payment popular in China in just a few years. From China's practices with regard to e-commerce, online consumption generates many insurance business scenarios for covering the risks entailed herein.

In summary, technology innovation, collectively reflected as FinTech at the current stage, generates new needs for innovative insurance products. From the supply side, insurance companies are keen to discover emerging and potential needs and accordingly provide corresponding insurance products for more profits and market shares.

2.3.1.3 Technology

FinTech enables insurance companies to "seamlessly" embed insurance services into their business links, including purchase, payment, and delivery, to meet customers' high-frequency and fragmented insurance needs more swiftly, conveniently, and at a lower cost. FinTech may also help companies improve their response speed to market changes and overall operation by equipping them with the ability to grasp the latest market dynamics, explore potential customers and adopt appropriate business strategies.

FinTech can support and improve insurance companies' business operations, products, and services. Therefore, insurance companies could leverage FinTech to improve their business efficiency, management level, and customer experience of them and their services, which ultimately promotes the progress of the insurance industry.

2.3.1.4 Concept

The in-depth application of FinTech in the insurance industry further highlights the "customer-centered" concept. The sales model is transforming from a product-centered to a customer-centered approach. The new sales model is one where FinTech no longer enables customers to passively accept the information presented by insurance companies. Instead, the new model's power lies in stimulating customer value in the sales process. In the future, the behavior data of customers will become an essential reference for insurance product design and service improvement.

2.3.2 FinTech Application in the Insurance Sector

2.3.2.1 The Usage of Big Data

Big Data is able to upgrade the insurance industry comprehensively. The Big Data era has witnessed a data explosion in the insurance industry. Nowadays, insurance companies have to process both structured and massive unstructured data. During their business operation, they face and process massive amounts of unstructured data in contracts, videos, images, graphics, invoices, text, spreadsheets, briefing files, and emails. By Big Data, the insurance industry could, upon leveraging massive structured and unstructured data, realize differentiated marketing, fully explore the value of their customers for personalized actuarial and product pricing, and expand their business coverage. With respect to risk control, Big Data can also effectively improve anti-fraud performance and reduce the customer complaint or suit likelihood for the insurance industry.

2.3.2.2 The Usage of Cloud Computing

Cloud Computing is to record innovative moments and accelerate the developments of the insurance industry. For example, insurance companies could use Cloud Computing to construct an "Insurance Cloud" for insurance companies and develop their core business modules, financial modules, and process management modules on the cloud, allowing their customers to complete insurance applications and complaints through the cloud, which is an excellent example to prove Cloud Computing's positive role in improving the customer service experience. Furthermore, in off-peak periods, they can lease their core, financial, and process management modules to create new profits.

2.3.2.3 Provide Opportunities for SMEs

During the FinTech transformation, insurance companies must invest a lot of resources and time in information infrastructure construction, system maintenance, and staff training. However, forse special investments are not cost-effective enough for small and medium-sized insurance companies. However, under Cloud Computing, they could borrow relevant platforms and equipment from suppliers or large insurance companies, where the cost of information platform construction could be saved for channel construction, product R&D, and customer experience.

2.3.2.4 Strengthen Information Sharing Within the Insurance Industry

- What can Cloud Computing do?

The advent of Cloud Computing makes building a nationwide unified insurance industry platform for information sharing feasible. We expect that, in China, in the future, based on Cloud Computing technology, local-level information-sharing platforms could integrate the data thereon into the unified platform to promote cross-industry data sharing and improve the service capability of insurance companies and the overall efficiency of the insurance industry.

- What can Blockchain do?

Blockchain is able to bring new thoughts to the development of the online insurance industry. First, it can reduce the risk of information asymmetry through its trust mechanism based on joint verification by online platforms, customers, physical examination institutions, hospitals, and other relevant traders, forming a complete insurance ecosystem. Customers' information and data regarding their physical condition, occupation, physical examination outcomes, and medical condition can be recorded and broadcast in due course through the whole network, subject to joint verification by the traders concerned, to ensure that the information or data is trustworthy and effective to reduce and mitigate the information asymmetry risk effectively.

Second, Blockchain can further reduce the cost for the insurance industry. Since Blockchain ensures established rules execute all transactions, the risk assessment is customized, and the underwriting cycle is shortened. Based on the Blockchain model, the insurance business, including underwriting and customer claims settlement, can operate without human intervention. This can effectively avoid dishonest behaviors such as fraud, reduce insurance costs and risks faced by most internet insurance platforms, and release the premium space.

Third, smart contract artifacts supported by Blockchain can be leveraged for smart contract insurance, which is automatically enforced by the code. Any trades can be quickly settled once specific conditions are met.

- What Internet of Things can do?

The Internet of Things can overturn the traditional business model of the insurance industry. With the development and popularity of wearable devices, the Internet of Things and modern medical technology are able to, by consolidating wearable devices, call centers, emergency centers, and medical facilities, build a remote health rescue service system that integrates a series of functions including prevention, monitoring, diagnosis, assistance and rehabilitation guidance, for patients to monitor their health status remotely without leaving their home or offices, so as to reduce their unnecessary times of hospital visits.

While health data is uploaded to the cloud and recorded electronically, the cloud platform can not only directly provide such data and corresponding analytical results (based on the data) to the patients but also send them to medical institutions upon their consent. The medical institutions will produce customized healthcare solutions, and smart health care occurs.

Based on the core database of the Internet of Things, insurance companies can realize real-time evaluation of the health status of policyholders based on wearable devices and conduct premium pricing and compensation support through Big Data analysis. With respect to property insurance, the application of the Internet of Things could also help insurance companies improve their precise pricing capacity and reduce the loss ratio for them. For example, insurance companies may provide their clients with smart home devices for free or at a low price, such as smart leak detectors and freezing alarms, which aim at helping their clients prevent home accidents so as to reduce the loss ratio covered by the property insurance they provide.

2.4 FinTech Promotes the Financial Industry

For now, the world is entering a new stage where economic development is highly driven by comprehensive information penetration and cross-border integration. In other words, the economic development model will be data-oriented in the future.

Financial business processes are constantly adjusted and optimized with the in-depth application and rapid iteration of digital technology. As a result, cross-industry and cross-market financial products are increasingly enriched in the financial market. Besides, converting different types of financial assets is more efficient, and financial activities' real-time and uninterrupted nature can be more salient.

As mentioned above, FinTech can be viewed as a product deeply integrating financial business and technology innovation. FinTech has produced a subtle impact on the realization of the financial function in modern society, the organization mode of the financial market, and the supply mode of financial services. Technically, FinTech further promotes integrated innovation, allocates financial resources into critical and weak areas in economic and social development, and helps to build the modern financial inclusion system where financial services are more accurate, technologies more advanced, financial service providers more responsible, and the development mode more sustainable, to meet the diversified needs of the real economy and massive customers, and to improve the efficiency of financial services and the financial market.

Nevertheless, there are multiple worries around FinTech as well. The development and application of FinTech, while making the financial division of labor more refined and the financial industry chain and value chain lengthened, has also led to many adverse outcomes for the financial industry. For example, the boundary between finance and technology turns from clear to blurred, and the responsible subjects and responsibilities regarding financial risk control and regulation are more challenging to identify and clarify (Tang et al. 2020).

2.4.1 *What Can FinTech Do for the Financial Industry*

2.4.1.1 Promote the Transformation and Upgrading of the Financial Industry

FinTech is to leverage modern technological achievements to optimize and innovate financial products and services, financial business models, and business processes. With the help of machine learning, data mining, and smart contract, financial institutions can simplify their interaction and dealing process with their customers and their counterparts, reducing the marginal financing cost and forming a new path to reach new customers. FinTech allows the continuous business optimization of financial institutions. It improves their core competitiveness regarding profit model, business form, assets and liabilities, credit management, and channel development, ultimately empowering the transformation and upgrading of the financial industry.

In recent years, the waves of FinTech have given birth to a number of new business models, including Direct Bank, online insurance, and Internet brokerage. The innovations of business models not only exert a considerable impact on the traditional business models but also force traditional financial institutions to change their traditional management modes and methods since they have to provide better financial products to meet the needs of the real economy and financial consumers, to maintain their market shares, i.e., to maintain competitiveness to emerging market players.

2.4.1.2 Bring the Financial Industry Back to Its Root—Serving the Real Economy

The finance is solely to be the intermediary of funds. FinTech allows the financial industry to swiftly capture the changes (especially on demand) in the digital economy market. By FinTech, we can conduct modeling analysis on the operation data of enterprises and real-timely monitor the capital flow, information flow, and logistics of relevant enterprises.

As such, it will be helpful to explore the scientific basis for the rational allocation of resources, to guide funds from overcapacity industries with high pollution and high energy consumption to emerging industries with high-tech and high value-added, and to serve the real economy. Furthermore, FinTech can be utilized to solve problems, including maturity mismatches of capital, pro-cyclical behaviors and the externalities of the financial network, and better to protect financial consumers' legitimate rights and interests.

2.4.1.3 Promote Digital Financial Inclusion to Eliminate the Digital Divide

FinTech can be an essential driving force for financial inclusion, effectively solving or mitigating the mismatch problem of high-cost financial services and low-income customers. FinTech helps financial institutions lower the service threshold, reduce the cost, and integrate financial services into the application scenarios of people's livelihoods.

In China, there are some remote areas where traditional financial services could be more convenient for local individuals and SMEs. For example, in some areas, many people may be without a bank account or a credit card. Fortunately, with the development of digital financial inclusion supported by FinTech, such problems can be effectively addressed. The reason is, FinTech is able to assist people in obtaining suitable financial support to overcome the high-cost and inconvenience problems faced by SME financing, as well as to strengthen financial support for the development of agriculture, rural areas, and rural residents, which contributes to breaking through the last constraints facing financial services, to improve the level of public service facilitation, and ultimately to promote the development of Digital Financial Inclusion.

Of course, the development of FinTech may also generate new problems. For example, it is difficult for low-income groups to adapt to the changes in financial service models brought about by the rapid development of FinTech. The resulting digital gap has become a new obstacle for these vulnerable groups to receive modern financial services. For another example, low-threshold credit services make it easier for young people who lack repayment ability to obtain loans, which leads to young people developing the habit of pre-expenditure and excessive consumption, causing a potential negative impact on financial stability.

2.4.1.4 A New Weapon to Prevent and Defuse Financial Risks

The rapid development of FinTech has promoted the digital transformation of financial markets and provided more financial regulation tools. Big Data, AI, and other technologies are used to establish financial risk control models to effectively identify high-risk transactions and intelligently perceive abnormal transactions so as to identify, warn and defuse the risk in advance and improve the capacity of technical defense against financial risks. For example, regarding shareholder access management, related transaction identification, and liquidity management, Big Data intelligent algorithms can scan enterprise risks around the financial condition, equity, correlation, and other information to realize the real-time analysis and handling of risks.

2.4.2 FinTech is Bringing Risks and Regulatory Challenges

The new characteristics and trends presented by FinTech in supply subject, innovative practice, financial risks, and consumer protection have posed a series of new challenges to the financial regulation system and regulation capacity.

2.4.2.1 Blur the Financial and Technological Attributes of the Market Players

In the field of FinTech, suppliers include not only traditional financial institutions that promote the transformation and upgrading of financial services through scientific and technological innovation but also Internet enterprises that use digital technology to carry out financial business across borders, as well as FinTech companies that provide outsourcing and supporting technical services for financial institutions.

These different types of institutions are becoming increasingly interconnected and interactive regarding accounts, products, channels, data, and infrastructure. For example, many data service providers in China regard themselves as technology companies whose business model is to provide multi-dimensional data-based credit evaluation services for bank loans, yet the essence is credit evaluation. For another example, some third-party network platforms, when providing insurance-related IT intermediary services, turn to operate illegal insurance intermediary businesses and carry out insurance agents in illegal and disguised ways, breeding some new types of illegal commercial insurance activities (Zhu 2016).

2.4.2.2 Difficult to Determine the Responsibilities in Case of Disputes

The informationization happening in China and the world has entered a new stage characterized by comprehensive penetration, cross-border integration, and leading development. Financial business processes are constantly optimizing and adjusting with the in-depth application and rapid iteration of digital technology. As a result, cross-industry and cross-market financial products are becoming more enriched, converting different types of financial assets more efficiently and making uninterrupted real-time attributes of financial activities more salient. However, these changes have reduced the effectiveness and customization of traditional financial governance. In the meantime, some technology companies apply for licenses to operate a financial business or cooperate with financial institutions. The financial industry chain and value chain are extended. Moreover, while the financial division of labor is more refined, the responsibility of risk control has become more complex and challenging to determine (Yang 2013).

2.4.2.3 Multiple Risks Overlap

FinTech makes the cross-integration and association penetration of different businesses more popular, which may produce the Domino Effect and Butterfly Effect of the cross-spread of multiple risks with respect to business, technology, and data. Regarding business risks, some institutions unilaterally pursue product innovation and the customer experience in the name of technological innovation to overpack the financial products and oversimplify necessary business processes and risk control links without guaranteeing the security of capital and transactions, causing significant security risks to the business. Regarding technical risk, some institutions blindly pursue the so-called disruptive technology, leading to the wrong selection, resource waste, and frequent security incidents. Furthermore, the financial industry increasingly depends on crucial information infrastructure such as servers, chips, and algorithms. As a result, a mistake in a supply chain node may be transmitted to the whole chain.

In terms of risks with regard to data, illegal behaviors of excessive data collection, data resale, and reuse in the FinTech field are expected. Nowadays, hackers can steal users' information through network attacks, Trojan viruses, SMS sniffing, and other means, making it urgent to pay attention to issues such as data leakage and privacy protection (Wu and Zhang 2015).

2.4.2.4 Bring Challenges to Financial Consumer Protection

With the help of efficient and ubiquitous network infrastructure, FinTech has lowered the threshold and reduced the cost of financial services, and extended financial services to the long tail customers such as the elderly and rural residents underserved by traditional financial institutions, promoting the development of Financial Inclusion.

However, at the same time, it is notable to mention that such long-tail customer groups often need higher digital financial literacy and more knowledge of finance and technology. Besides, their understanding, acceptance, adaptability and risk identification, and bearing ability of FinTech must be improved, making it easier for them to grasp all kinds of intelligent products and services flexibly. It may also cause them to uphold the concept that all investments are without risks blindly. Moreover, in the context of the financial industry's digital transformation, consumers are often at a technical and information disadvantage. Their personal identical and financial information is excessively collected, increasing the difficulty of protecting their legitimate rights and interests.

According to statistics, as of March 2020, the number of China's non-Internet users was 496 million, 51.6% of whom do not surf the Internet because of the need for network skills. Furthermore, according to the survey data from the Financial Consumer Protection Bureau of the PBOC, the national consumer financial literacy index in 2021 was 66.81, which still has much room for improvement.

References

Hauswald RBH, Marquez RS (2003) Information technology and financial services competition. Rev Financ Stud 3(16)

Jin H, Li H, Liu Y (2020) Financial technology, bank risk and market crowding-out effect. Financ Res (05)

Qiu H, Huang Y, Ji Y (2018) The impact of FinTech on traditional banking behavior from the perspective of Internet finance. Financ Res (11)

Tang S, Wu X, Zhu J (2020) Digital finance and enterprise technology innovation-structural characteristics, mechanism identification and effect differences under financial supervision. Manag World (05)

World Bank (2016) World bank development report: digital dividends. World Bank, Washington, DC

Wu X, Zhang X (2015) Risk characteristics and regulatory suggestions of pure network banks in China. Tsinghua Financ Rev (08)

Xie Z, Zhao Xi, Liu Y (2018) Fintech development and digital strategic transformation of commercial banks. China Soft Sci (08)

Yang Q (2013) Research on the special risks and prevention of internet finance in China. Financ Technol Era (07)

Zhu T (2016) Research on potential risks and regulatory responses. Res Financ Regul (55)

Chapter 3
The Rise of BigTechs in the Financial Market

Introduction

At an early stage, western media regarded Google, Amazon, Facebook, and Apple as "Four BigTechs" and later included Microsoft and referred to them as "Five BigTechs". However, as time passes, the word "BigTech" is currently more often used to refer to large technology companies with a wide range of business scopes and massive influence in relevant markets. Pursuant to this definition, in China, several large Internet enterprises, including Alibaba, Baidu, Tencent, Etc., also fall into the scope of BigTech.

In a paper on banking supervision released by the Basel Committee in 2017, BigTechs were defined as large global technology companies with huge advantages of digital technology. For example, they can directly provide search engines, e-commerce, and IT platform with data storage and processing functions, Etc., for their customers or provide infrastructure services for other companies. In April 2019, the Bank for International Settlements (the "BIS") provided in its working paper that BigTech referred to technology giants with great user and technology bases and could enter the financial market in a short time.

3.1 Nature and Features of BigTech

With respect to the provision of financial services, BigTechs have a unique business strategy to kick off their financial expansion, starting with the payment business. BigTechs prefer to provide payment services by virtue of existing infrastructures and then expand their service scope to other financial business areas, including credit, insurance, savings, and investment, independently or cooperating with financial institutions.

According to the BIS (2019), the business model of BigTech relies on three key factors, i.e., data, network, and activity. These three factors complement each other

D. Zhao et al., *FinTech and SupTech in China*, Contributions to Finance and Accounting,
https://doi.org/10.1007/978-981-99-5173-4_3

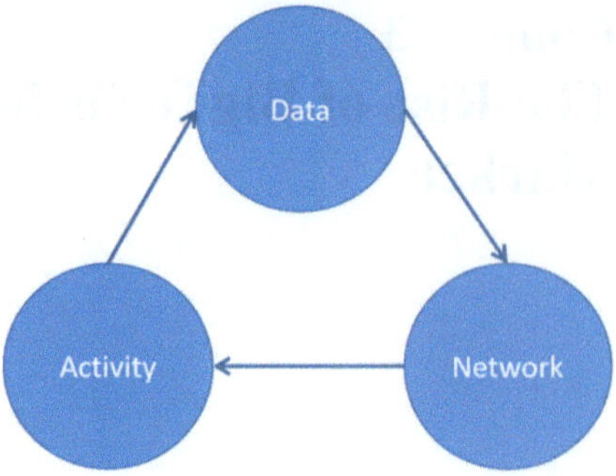

Fig. 3.1 Three key factors for BigTech business model. *Data source* The bank for international settlements (2019)

(see Fig. 3.1). Among them, the network refers to the platform run by BigTech, benefiting the users thereon by providing them with more transaction opportunities as increasing buyers and sellers participate. The network is to bring more users into the platform and create value for them. In specific, BigTech may continuously keep mining data and thereby provide a wide range of services under the network effect to generate more user activities and more data to expand the platform.

Based on the positive circulation of data, network, and activity given in Fig. 3.1, a number of Chinese BigTechs are engaging in or preparing to provide financial products and services, including but not limited to payments, fund management, insurance, credit, Etc. With respect to revenue distribution of BigTechs, the majority comes from consulting services based on information technology, e.g., Cloud Computing and data analytics. For most Bigtechs, their core business is closely related to FinTech and might account for approximately 46% of the total revenue, while the revenue from financial business accounts for around 11%, which is only a small fraction of their global business.

However, given the business scale and customer volume of BigTech, the engagement of BigTech in the financial industry might lead to changes to the financial market, which is challenging to regulators and risky to the market as well as the consumers therein. Therefore, global BigTechs serving users around the world might prefer Asia–Pacific and North America. A recent report released by the BIS provided that BigTech had widest participation in the financial business in China and had gradually aimed at other emerging economies like Southeast Asia, East Africa and Latin America.

Baidu, Alibaba, Tencent, and JingDong are four Internet platform giants in China for the time being, and have, through greenfield or brownfield investments, established their FinTech subsidies, i.e., Du Xiaoman Finance, Ant Financial, Tencent FiT and JingDong Finance respectively. From a business perspective, they can be referred to as the Chinese four BigTechs. Regarding financial market participation, they could fully leverage their platform ecosystem advantages and provide financial services featuring technology innovation.

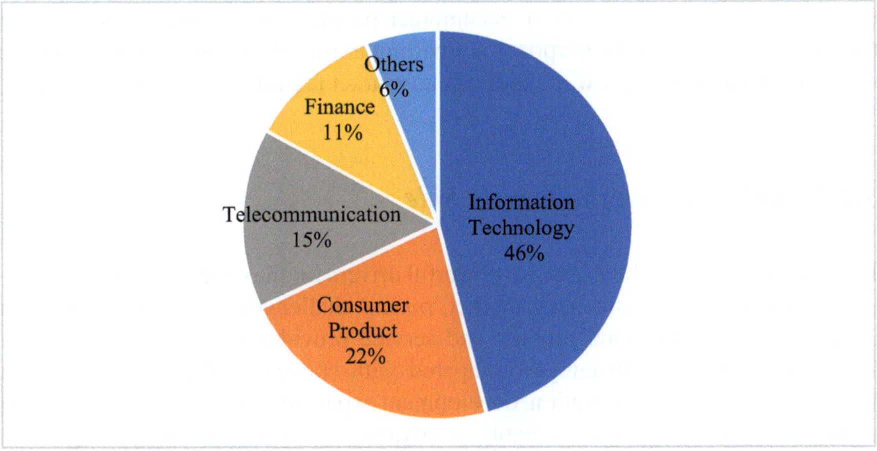

Fig. 3.2 Revenue distribution of BigTech. *Note* Samples include alibaba, slphabet, amazon, apple, baidu, facebook, grab, kakao, mercado libre, lotte, samsung, and tencent. "Others" include healthcare, real estate, and infrastructures. *Data source* S&P Capital IQ, BIS

Massive users and data generated on a platform could create significant economic value for the platform operator, which is a BigTech in most cases. Moreover, the platform operator is in the core position in the platform economy since it is responsible for connecting all other parties engaged in the platform. In other words, the platform operator consolidates various links along the economic chain, covering production, circulation, and consumption, which is beneficial to addressing the problem of fund surplus or fund shortage (Fig. 3.2).

3.2 Drivers of BigTech Providing Financial Services

3.2.1 Drivers from the Demand Side

From the demand side, in China, there are actual needs of consumers for financial services provided by BigTech. Over the past two decades, the financial industry has undergone rapid development. However, financial service by traditional financial institutions is not accessible to many people, especially in rural areas, where many farmers even have no bank account or credit card, let alone other financial services. In this regard, BigTech could fill this gap to promote financial inclusion by providing innovative financial services. The role of BigTech is particularly outstanding in emerging markets and developing economies.

Furthermore, the existence of consumer preference also promotes the rise of BigTech in the financial market. Consumers and small enterprises prefer the financial products from BigTech, especially the younger generation, which is more likely to favor technological innovation and embrace business improvement. Moreover, in China, many people and enterprises are willing to reform business, so BigTech has solid ground to further grow in the financial market regarding the demand side.

3.2.2 *Drivers from the Supply Side*

From the supply side, there are also powerful drivers for the development and expansion of BigTech in the financial market, posing challenges to traditional financial institutions. As a financial product and service provider in the financial market, BigTech has various advantages compared with conventional regulated financial institutions concerning operation, development expansion, and marketing, including significant data advantage, technology advantage, capital advantage, regulatory environment advantage, and competition environment advantage.

3.2.2.1 Data Advantage

Unlike traditional financial institutions focusing on financial business, BigTech has many other business scenarios that provide BigTech with more consumer interactions. Furthermore, the core of BigTech is "Tech" rather than finance, which means that BigTech is much more experienced with regard to data collection and further utilization than most financial institutions. In summary, the data advantage of BigTech is the broader access to massive customer data and more advanced data analysis technology.

With respect to data capability, BigTech is able to extract quality data from various business scenarios and conduct further analysis, which allows BigTech to assess the credit status and risk profile of consumers (e.g., loan borrowers and policyholders) in financial transactions to achieve more accurate assessment outcomes and reduce the cost.

3.2.2.2 Technology Advantage

As mentioned above, whilst financial institutions focus on financial business, BigTech focuses more on technology and therefore is naturally more familiar with emerging technologies, including AI and Machine Learning, Etc., which are the foundation of data analysis and user screening capabilities that matter in the current transformation of the financial market.

3.2.2.3 Fund Advantage

In the past years, BigTechs have had more discretion on funds than strictly regulated commercial banks. A relatively loose regulatory environment allows BigTechs to absorb raw funds through various channels, including but not limited to:

- Equity investments
- Asset-Backed Securities (the “ABS”)
- Partnerships with commercial banks
- Establish their banks.

3.2.2.4 Advantages Regarding Regulatory Environment

BigTech is an outcome of innovation usually ahead of the laws and regulations. In other words, in most cases, laws and regulations must catch up to the progress of the era, as innovation (especially technical innovation) is hard to expect.

In the early stages, financial laws and regulations did not cover BigTech providing financial services, creating competitive advantages and leading to the concentration of risks.

3.2.2.5 Advantages Regarding Competition Environment

Competition among commercial banks and other traditional institutions is reasonably sufficient in China. In contrast, BigTech has a high market concentration rate. In other words, it is convenient for BigTech to enter the financial market and eat market share from traditional financial institutions by providing technology-supported financial services. Besides, since the number of BigTechs in the market is quite limited, BigTechs are also convenient to reach monopoly status in their intended or agreed separated market and conduct new types of monopolistic activities, for example, data monopoly.[1]

[1] Frost J, Gambacorta L, Huang Y, Shin HS, Zbinden P (Apr 2019) BigTech and the changing structure of financial intermediation, BIS Working Papers, No 779.

3.3 Positive Aspects of BigTech to the Financial Industry

3.3.1 Improve the Quality of Financial Services and Promote Financial Inclusion

BigTech may significantly improve the quality of financial services in the financial market. The technology advantage allows BigTech to provide financial services at lower cost and beyond physical restrictions to many underserved areas. That being said, BigTechs is technically convenient to expand their business to remote areas and provide financial services for numerous underserved populations.

The payment service is a case in point. As mentioned above, the payment business is usually the first choice for BigTech to start its expansion plan in the financial market. The payment service mainly addresses the trust starving between buyers and sellers on e-commerce platforms, where the buyer hopes to receive the goods. In contrast, the seller hopes to deliver the goods after receiving the money from the buyer due to the need for more trust in each other. The third-party payment platform is to address this trust issue by providing temporary custody of purchase money to both parties until the goods are delivered. Alipay (run by Alibaba) and (PayPal run by eBay) are two influential third-party platforms in China. For areas with underdeveloped local retail payment system, online payment service provided by mobile network operators is able to reach residents whose access to traditional financial services had been cut off by geographical restrictions before, such as M-Pesa in several African countries. In China, online payment services by BigTech serve as an excellent alternative to traditional electronic payment tools by commercial banks, such as credit and debit cards. Besides, the online payment business model is cost-effective for BigTech to make market expansions, provide quality services and ultimately promote the progress of financial inclusion.

The Financial Stability Board (the "FSB") (2020) provided in its research paper that, among others, BigTech tends to expand faster and broader in emerging markets than in developed markets with regard to financial services provision. This is because financial inclusion is relatively lower in emerging markets, especially in rural areas inhabited by low-income people and need more financial services. The popularity of mobile phones and the Internet has laid the foundation for BigTech to enter the financial market and expand further.[2]

In the field of credit business, BigTech can actively carry out microfinance business to promote the continuous sinking of service focus and improve the availability of their financial services. It is estimated that in 2019, the credit business scale created by FinTech companies and BigTechs would reach in the region of USD800 billion, with FinTech companies accounting for $223 billion and BigTechs accounting for USD572 billion. The credit business scale outside the traditional banking system is

[2] FSB (Oct 2020) BigTech Firms in Finance in Emerging Market and Developing Economies-Market developments and Potential Financial Stability Implications. https://www.fsb.org/wp-content/uploads/P121020-1.pdf.

expected to be a beneficial supplement rather than a simple replacement since the scale is created by additional channels for credit services instead of original channels replacement.[3]

For online credit business operations, BigTechs usually adopt three methods, including:

- Develop the online banking model dependently. However, remote (i.e., online) bank account openings might be restricted by some regulators.
- Cooperate with traditional commercial banks. In this model, BigTechs are responsible for the loan facilitation related to approval based on their customer base and Big Data technologies. Commercial banks are responsible for the loan release and management.
- Seek funds through a joint loan or the ABS. This method was once widely adopted by FinTech companies. The total ABS amount released by Ant Financial in 2017 accounts for nearly 1/3 of the total in China. According to the Bank for International Settlements (the "BIS"), countries may vary in the growth rate of credit business by FinTech companies, which is decided by the economic growth differences among countries and their respective financial market structures. Generally speaking, the per capita income of residents of a country is negatively related to the traditional banking system competitiveness of the country and is positively related to the FinTech credit business scale.[4]

3.3.2 Promote the Competition and Cooperation in the Financial Sector

3.3.2.1 Complementary Relations Between BigTech and Financial Institutions

In China and beyond, BigTech and traditional financial institutions have a close cooperation relationship thanks to their complementary roles, apart from their fierce competitive relationship as introduced above.

The advantage of FinTech companies lies in their technology base. Compared with traditional financial institutions, FinTech companies have more technical resources and more powerful technological tools like AI and Big Data, which allow them to optimize their internal management process, business process, and interactions with customers. For example, Big Data analysis allows FinTech companies to serve customers through more flexible methods (e.g., online support) and provide tailored financial services for customers based on the analysis of their behavior data. BigTech is more powerful both in customer base and technology base than general FinTech

[3] Cornelli G, Frost J, Gambacorta L, Rau R, Wardrop R, Ziegler T (Sep 2020) FinTech and BigTech credit: a new database. BIS Working Papers, No 887.

[4] BIS (Jun 2019) Bigtech in finance: opportunities and risks. BIS Annual Economic Report. https://www.bis.org/publ/arpdf/ar2019e3.pdf.

companies, and is able to use a series of more powerful Big Data and AI tools through its robust networks and numerous customer data generated thereon. With respect to the development and operation cost, due to the high digitalization, the marginal cost of its services can be minimized to nearly zero.

The advantage of traditional financial institutions lies in their rich experience in various financial businesses and the corresponding industrial reputation and customer base generated therein, with which BigTech cannot catch up in the short term.

A sound and relatively perfect FinTech ecology require a cooperative model where FinTech companies and traditional financial institutions can complement their advantages to achieve mutual benefits and win–win results. For example, FinTech companies may provide technical services or technical support for traditional financial institutions, streamline processes, innovate models and upgrade services of traditional financial businesses with modern information technologies, develop new business areas that cannot be covered by traditional finance, and ultimately more profound the division of work within the financial sector.

Another example is that BigTech, whilst competing with traditional commercial banks in the payment service, still highly relies on the latter. In the e-commerce business, third-party payment platforms like Alipay and WeChat Pay, when engaged in the online payment business, need to contract with commercial banks for the payment and settlement system and connect their customers to their cooperative commercial banks for transaction completion through the interfaces of the banks.

In areas of wealth management and insurance, Etc., some BigTechs are trying to undertake the distribution channels for commercial banks, securities companies, or insurance companies by linking financial products and services to their powerful online platforms and their vast customer networks.

3.3.2.2 Competition Relations Between BigTech and Financial Institutions

BigTech may leverage its outstanding technology services to venture into the financial sector and export financial services to the financial market. Therefore, there might be potential conflicts of interest as BigTech are also a competitor to financial institutions. In particular, developing online platforms brings platform advantage and data advantage for BigTech. In addition, it enables BigTech to interact with customers directly and to provide more tailored and humanized financial services, which would undoubtedly cause enormous external competition pressure on traditional financial institutions, mainly traditional commercial banks.

Apple, Google, Facebook, Alibaba, and Tencent are leveraging their vast customer base and common user interfaces, including smartphones, social networks, chat robots, Etc., to access the banking system. They collect more data and information regarding the needs and profiles of customers in order to provide a comprehensive service experience for their customers, which would not only completely change the traditional methods of payment and settlement via cash, bank card, credit card, Etc., but also affect the retail business of commercial banks. For example, BigTech may provide one-stop shopping for a series of financial products through online platforms, which is more convenient and efficient for customers than the original model of traditional commercial banks or other financial institutions.

3.3.3 Different Impact of BigTech on the Financial Industry

The influence of FinTech startups and BigTechs on the financial industry might vary from each other. FinTech startups can become game changers in the field of finance. It replicates the customer-centered culture of the Internet industry in the financial industry, effectively lowering the financing threshold and costs. However, the influence of FinTech startups on the existing banking system is limited. Besides, they might be acquired by traditional financial institutions represented by commercial banks or compete with financial institutions in partial market segments (e.g., equity crowdfunding).

In contrast, the influence of BigTech on the financial market could be huge, especially in the payment service market. For example, Amazon Pay operates across ten countries, Google Pay across 22 countries, and Apple Pay across 25 countries. Alipay and WeChat Pay nearly occupy a monopoly position in the domestic third-party payment market. In addition, unlike FinTech startups, BigTech has already had a large business scale, client base, and powerful technology capability, and therefore tends to own abundant financial resources, strong brand awareness, global customer base, and access to cutting-edge technology, which makes BigTech more capable of integrating the resources with the entire financial services sector into a digital ecosystem to redefine the traditional financial intermediary business. Moreover, BigTech also has a strong network effect, which would further increase the market concentration or even cause monopolies where large conglomerates would benefit the most rather than the financial market or the public.[5]

3.3.4 Risks and Challenges Behind BigTech

BigTech, whilst bringing a series of benefits to the financial market and the public, including improving the efficiency of financial services as well as the quality of financial products, and promoting financial inclusion, leads to a new series of financial market risks and regulatory challenges, against which regulators around the globe should be cautious.

[5] Beau D (Jan 2019) Financial regulation and supervision issues raised by the impact of tech firms on financial services, Speech at the ESSEC, Paris. https://www.bis.org/review/r190130a.html.

3.3.5 Monopoly and Anti-Competition Activities

BigTech is able to acquire additional data in addition to regular data generated from their own ecosystem including social networks, searches, and e-commerce platforms. The growth of data category and scale enables BigTech to get extra benefits. For example, extra data of individual customers (e.g., credit scores) collected beyond regular business scenarios would have more excellent value when combined with specific existing data or data groups. In addition, they would produce economies of scale effects when applied by BigTech in its financial products and services to provide for a more comprehensive population range.

Given the above, the potential value of customer data can be crucially advantageous for BigTech, whilst remaining less meaningful or meaningless to other subjects, even concerned customers. For example, if customers of commercial banks permit BigTech with unrestricted access to their data in the banking system or even sell their data for direct or indirect profits, the DNA (Data, Network, and Activity) loop, as introduced in Fig. 3.1 would be constantly strengthened, further promoting the competitive advantage of BigTech to overwhelm the banks. Moreover, once BigTech has completed constructing its ecosystem in exclusiveness, its potential competitors in the concerned market would need more room to build a similar platform for competition. Even worse, BigTech may prevent or wipe out potential or existing competition by excluding or merging potential competitors, which would result in a "winner-take-all" situation, which is detrimental to the financial market development and the interests of massive financial consumers.

Platform advantage can significantly form and enhance the market monopoly position of BigTech, which will leverage its market forces and network externalities to increase customers' switching costs, reinforcing its monopoly status. For example, Apple, Amazon, and Facebook are trying to consolidate their power in the payment market through acquisitions, partnerships, Etc. In addition, BigTech may also adopt other anti-competition conducts to maintain its market status, undermine competitors, and prevent potential competitors, including but not limited to bundle sales[6] and cross-subsidization. Therefore, BigTech may, based on the advantages mentioned above and conducts, enjoy excessively concentrated power regarding resource allocation, Etc., and may gradually develop into a market monopolizer.

Moreover, regulators should also pay attention to the data monopoly phenomenon that BigTech may cause. In the era of digital economy, the scale, diversification, and update rate of data grow exponentially, and the value of data increases as well. It is pronounced for the financial industry, which is data-intensive due to the nature of financial business. In recent years, the value of data has been constantly discovered, proved, and applied in the financial sector, promoting the reform and optimization of

[6] Bundle sales is a marketing strategy where companies combine two or more products into one product and sell it at a discount, cheaper than the total amount of all products, while consumers buy these products alone. Bundle sales can be regarded as a particular form of price discrimination, usually in multi-product industries such as telecommunications, hardware and software, and is inconsistent with the competition regulation.

the operation logic, operation model, and management manner of financial business.[7] Through Big Data-related technologies, BigTech can collect, organize and arrange the data left by users to analyze users' consumption habits and form their portraits. Through massive business scenarios and platform advantages, BigTech masters a vast amount of microdata and information and may further process and analyze the data and information with its information technologies, to provide comprehensive and considerate information services and tailored financial services for the users so as to increase the user stickiness to the platform of BigTech. There are significant potential benefits behind the user stickiness, from which BigTech may acquire a lot of extra profits, such as advertising revenue.

In the era of the digital economy, the one who owns and holds more data would be more likely to be in a favorable position in the fierce market competition. Furthermore, BigTech is able to, by virtue of its customer base and technical advantages, collect a large amount of data at a cost near to zero, thereby creating a "data monopoly" for itself.[8] Once BigTech establishes its data-dominant role in a market, it can discriminate against prices and squeeze rent. Especially in the credit business, BigTech may not only use relevant data to assess the credibility level of a potential borrower but also determine the highest loan rate the borrower is willing to pay, which means, BigTech would clearly understand the bottom line of its customers and thereby maximize its profit, which is harmful to the welfare of both customers and the market.[9]

Price discrimination by BigTech has been a severe problem facing Chinese consumers and has already attracted the attention of Chinese regulators. Price discrimination increases the profits of BigTech at customers' expense without changing the total volume of production and consumption and will negatively affect social welfare. Take the insurance industry as an example. As a result, BigTech may exclude high-risk groups from the insurance market.

3.3.6 Issues on Data Abuse and Consumer Protection

BigTech engaged in financial business will cause the centralized collection and exposure of various financial and non-financial information of massive consumers, which means BigTech can acquire not only social, shopping, and web browsing data and information of users but also the data and information concerning their bank accounts, payment records, deposits, withdrawals, holdings and transaction records of financial

[7] LI W (2021) Improve data governance and strengthen privacy protection. Tsinghua Financial Review (1).

[8] Stucke M (2018) Should we be concerned about data-opolies?. Georg Law Technol Rev 2(2). https://www.fsb.org/wp-content/uploads/P121020-1.pdf. Accessed 12 October 2020.

[9] Bar-Gill O (2019) Algorithmic price discrimination when demand is a function of both preferences and (mis) perceptions. Univ Chic Law Rev 86 (2).

assets, Etc. Besides, BigTech can connect the information with biological information through facial recognition, health monitoring, and other ways. Worse, any data leakage incidents resulting from improper storage or network attacks, Etc., could harm customers' privacy and lead to property losses, even physical damages, as their accurate profile would be easily identified with minor analysis.

According to the Statistical Report on China's Internet Development released by the China Internet Network Information Center, as of June 2020, more than 20% of Chinese netizens had suffered from personal information leakage. Most information leakage and malicious marketing incidents result from information abuse and Big Data discrimination. In theory, these incidents will seriously infringe on the rights and interests of financial consumers, including their right to know, right to choose, and right to privacy, Etc.

Meanwhile, Big Data, AI, and other similar technologies can easily lead to "algorithmic discrimination," which will seriously damage the interests of particular groups. Compared with traditional discrimination behaviors, algorithmic discrimination is more difficult to restrain, especially when the target is large internet enterprises that own massive data of hundreds of millions of consumers. From the micro perspective, BigTech may legitimately acquire or use the data with due authorization. However, from a macro perspective, since data has partial public nature, the legitimacy and boundary issue over data management and data process should not be viewed only as an individual issue that can be addressed by individual authorization but also as an issue concerning the financial market and social welfare. So far, the concepts of "data owner" and "data ownership" have still been controversial.

3.3.7 Excessive Consumption and Data Mining

Targeted marketing based on data mining has become a critical business model for many online platforms. Larger online platforms operated by BigTech are able to accurately send various kinds of marketing information to users according to their daily behavior data. In most cases, the marketing information sent by online platforms is related to the cooperative companies or affiliates of the platforms. The relevant platform will charge a service fee for cooperative companies for flow provision. However, in some cases, driven by commercial interests, some large internet platforms may excessively track and collect users' digital footprints and improperly implement data-driven marketing strategies.

The most valuable part of digital footprints is the financial data of individual users, including their accounts, transaction, credit information, Etc. BigTech is motivated to mine the users' financial behavior and analyze the characteristics thereof, and accordingly push financial marketing advertisements niche targeting to the platform users. The marketing strategy supported by data mining popularizes the concepts of excessive consumption and consumption with debts, Etc. It makes such concepts more and more acceptable to people with poor credit.[10] Unfortunately, it is difficult for financial consumers to distinguish the risks behind targeted marketing that may undermine consumers' legal rights and interests. It will be even more difficult for customers to defend their rights and interests against actual infringements.

3.3.8 BigTech's Impact on Financial Stability and Systemic Risks

There are specific platforms under BigTech responsible for providing users with various financial services. Enjoying the broad participation of massive users and operating as holdings, these platforms increase the possibility of communication among various risks across multiple markets and sectors. However, if BigTechs are continuously kept free from regulation and supervision and not restrained by the financial safety net, serious risk contagion and systemic financial risks might be produced quickly if any risk exposures occur.

3.3.8.1 Risks from Long-Tail Customers

As mentioned above, one of the benefits brought by BigTech is that it cares for and serves the long-tail customers underserved by traditional financial institutions. However, it should also be noted that such customers are more likely to lack professional financial knowledge and decision capabilities related to investments and tend to be in group psychology.

Given the above, the long-tail customers might behave over-irrationally for market fluctuations or when market conditions are reversed, which will lead to the proliferation and spread of long-tail risks, and may further develop into a systemic financial risk.

3.3.8.2 Systemic Operation Risks

The network scale effect and the centralization of technical services would produce systemic operation risks more easily. In China, the market concentration of third-party cloud services is relatively high. The combined market share of the top three service providers, Alibaba, Tencent, and Huawei, is over 90%.

In the future, financial institutions need to cooperate with these third-party cloud service providers to build cloud platforms. Since the third-party cloud service market is highly concentrated, any single operation failure, network failure, or other risk events of one cloud service provider could cause large-scale operational failures

[10] Research Group of the Financial Consumer Protection Bureau of the PBOC (2021) Research on consumer financial information protection under large Internet platforms. Studies of the PBOC (4).

and network security risks to quantities of financial institutions, which might even spread the failures or risks to other institutions. Then a systemic operation risk would occur. For example, the crash of Ali Cloud in March 2019 caused many websites and applications of internet companies using Ali Cloud services to be paralyzed.

3.3.8.3 Enhanced Infectivity and Procyclicality of Financial Risks

Due to the extensive use of Big Data, Cloud Computing, and other network information technologies by BigTech, the convergence of business models and algorithms enhances the infectivity and procyclicality of financial risks. The development and application of financial software are based on massive financial data. Suppose the market of financial data suppliers is highly concentrated. In that case, massive users are likely to use the same or similar algorithm strategy to assist them in investing, which would cause the investment decisions around the market to be highly consistent.

In extreme occasions, many investors would simultaneously get the same or similar latest information and updates regarding the market and accordingly make the same or similar investment decisions, which might cause rapid changes in the price of corresponding investment targets. When the price of the investment target is suddenly raised, other auxiliary decision software would quickly find the "upward trend" and adopt the "chase up" strategy. The opposite will happen in the decline of the price. It will lead to the herd effect of investment behavior, exacerbating the pro-cyclical nature of the financial market.[11]

3.3.8.4 Blurred Boundaries

Cross-industry and cross-field financial products advocated by BigTech, could be interlaced with each other and cause blurred boundaries among various financial products and businesses, as well as further risk concealment and destruction.

For traditional financial institutions, financial services must meet the qualification requirements specified by laws and regulations, adhere to the principle of licensed operation, and strictly enforce access administration and business supervision. However, large internet companies represented by BigTech are not subject to these requirements for carrying out financial businesses by claiming to be pure technology companies. In that case, they may not only evade regulation but also be free from disorderly expansion, which would cause market risks and undermine the regulatory goals of fair competition and consumer protection.

In addition, traditionally, even if financial products and services are provided in greater varieties, there are still clear boundaries under the traditional framework with firewalls, and corresponding regulatory requirements are relatively straightforward.

[11] WANG Q (2019) Analysis on Several Relationships in the Development of the FinTech. Journal of Finance and Economics (5)

However, the intervention of BigTech and the application of innovative technologies have changed the structure, function, and nature of quantities of financial products and services to a considerable extent, resulting in the blurred boundaries among and confusing nature of these financial products and services, which would give the possibility of regulatory arbitrage for relevant entities.

3.3.9 *How to Effectively Regulate BigTech?*

When it comes to the effective regulation of BigTechs, it is necessary to pay great attention to their huge customer base, information acquisition channels, and business models, and by learning from the regulation, competition policy, and data privacy supervision for regulated financial institutions, establish a comprehensive regulatory framework. What is more, the attention of relevant regulators should also be paid to fair competition, consumer rights and interests, market access, Etc. At the same time, since BigTech tends to operate across regulatory and geographical boundaries, cross-border regulatory coordination also matters.

3.3.10 *Re-examine the Relationship Between Competition and Financial Stability*

There have been two views on market access to the banking industry. One view is that new companies entering the banking industry can effectively promote competition, so the access threshold of the banking sector should be relaxed to encourage new companies to enter. The other view is that moderate concentration or low competitiveness in the banking sector is desirable. Moreover, it will benefit financial stability because it can make bank shareholders more profitable and more likely to be cautious, so the banking barriers to access should be tightened.

However, the actual impacts of BigTech's entry into the financial industry on the financial market competition go beyond the expectation given by both above two views. BigTech can independently complete the DNA flow described in Fig. 3.1 through its advantages in Big Data analysis, network externalities, and interaction. The positive DNA cycle could connect market competition and data flow well.

Moreover, BigTechs may establish and consolidate various market forces through their controls on critical digital platforms, including e-commerce, search, and social networking platforms. When BigTechs and financial institutions have tight business reliance rely on these platforms, BigTech's control on key platforms might cause direct conflicts of interest and reduce competition within the financial market.

Last but not least, huge user network and external network effects allow BigTechs to be able to establish dominance within relevant markets in a short time, which means, BigTechs may become monopolistic institutions in relevant markets they locate and further increase the concentration rate of such markets shortly after their engagements, which is a detriment to both orderly market competition and financial stability.

3.3.11 Provide Fair and Transparent Regulation

3.3.11.1 Uphold Equality in Financial Regulation

Although the business model and operation logic of BigTechs and traditional financial institutions vary from each other, the attributes of the financial products they provide remain the same or similar. However, as mentioned above, BigTech has some overwhelming advantages in some key aspects, which will cause a series of corresponding risks to the financial industry and the public. Therefore, a new regulatory framework should be established to address such issues and provide a fair competition environment for various financial market participants so as to address the competition distortion effectively, and BigTechs might bring potential risks to the financial market.

Therefore, the principle of regulatory consistency should be adhered to in the regulation of BigTechs and formal financial institutions. In other words, under a relatively ideal financial regulatory framework, all of the different entities should be regulated according to related factors, including their conducts, market powers, and market risks, Etc., rather than their outer forms.

Specifically, for financial market engagement, BigTech should be equally regulated financial institutions to apply and hold valid financial licenses corresponding to their business and be subject to the look-through regulation, functional regulation, and the principle of "substance over form". Besides, financial regulators should keep their regulatory policies, business rules, and standards consistent over various entities to prevent regulatory arbitrage (Sun 2017).

3.3.11.2 Include BigTechs into the Macro-Prudential Regulation System

BigTech operates a wide range of businesses and has large stake groups and strong spillovers. In this regard, the regulators should be able to understand the nature and business attributes of BigTech at the level same or similar to their knowledge of financial institutions and, on this basis, conduct macro-prudential regulation on them by reference to large systemic financial institutions or financial holding groups with the common regulatory topic as "too big to fail". In this regard, BigTech would be imposed strict regulatory requirements regarding capital adequacy ratio, asset-liability ratio, and information disclosure.

Since there are some gaps between BigTech and regulated financial institutions with regard to their business model, for the consistency of regulation, the existing regulatory index regime should include both micro and macro-prudential index systems with BigTech covered. BigTech should also comply with additional obligations for their different characteristics and risks. For example, they ensure the security of their technologies and establish and constantly perfect the firewall system to prevent the crossover and transfer of risks.

In a word, the existing regulatory framework should be continuously improved to provide legal support for strengthening the regulation of BigTech, and increasing penalties for BigTech's violations of laws and regulations.

3.3.11.3 Strengthen Data Regulation and Privacy Protection

Data itself is a non-competitive commodity since it can be widely used without loss and obtained at zero marginal cost as a byproduct of services for BigTech. The free sharing of data is socially desirable. In a fully competitive market, opening data access could help reduce the cost of customer conversion and promote competition and financial inclusion.

The key is how to promote and realize data sharing. Data's value can only be produced with the efficient and orderly circulation of data elements. Therefore, formulating and implementing regulatory rules covering data flow management and privacy protection and selectively allowing the sharing of certain types of data would effectively reduce the extra competitive advantages of BigTech created by its large-scale database, which is beneficial to promote fair competition within relevant markets.

Some countries and regions have established relevant rules on data sharing and privacy protection. For example, the European Union and the United Kingdom have formulated policies and measures to promote the development of open banking, which allows authorized third-party financial service providers to directly access customer data from commercial banks, which are also provided with peer access to the data from the third-party providers. However, there are still some difficulties regarding the use of data.

First, the right to data is hard to determine and is under great controversy for now. Financial institutions, e-commerce platforms and internet companies collect a large amount of data when carrying out their business activities, covering authorized data, unauthorized data, behavior trace data, and associated derivative data, Etc. Nevertheless, there still needs to be a forceful legal basis for defining the ownership and interests of data from the legislative perspective.

Second, data ownership is hard to divide and allocate for different subjects since data is easy to retain and can be repeatedly copied and transferred. Third, the ownership and control of data can be transferred through data sharing. Data transfer of data processors has been a common concern for regulators around the globe, and in recent years, Chinese laws and regulations have tried to address this issue.

Third, the value of data is challenging to measure. Data elements are different from traditional production factors. Data is non-physical and virtual, making it difficult to measure data usage. Furthermore, it is not easy to measure the value of data merely from the volume because data is in diverse dimensions and has various connotations and complex structures.[12]

Data is an important right or interest for the customers concerned, and therefore financial consumer protection is an issue closely related to data regulation and privacy protection. The elegant balance between data regulation and personal information protection is vital in preventing the occurrence of data monopoly. Legislative efforts should address the financial consumer and investor protection, interpret the ownership or at least relevant interests of data elements, and provide the criteria for determining the rights and interests related to data, the subjects concerned, and their rights and obligations. In particular, it is necessary to clarify the legal attributes and right or interest boundaries of the numerous consumer data in the hands of BigTechs. Fair and reasonable allocation of data production factors is vital to prevent the occurrence of data monopoly and the excessive profits obtained therein. Regulators should, in addition to the strict control of data abuse,

- Encourage data opening and data sharing under legitimacy, including promoting the sharing of public data, desensitized data held by financial institutions, and any other data legally allowable for sharing.
- Ensure the data be invisible and measurable when used. In addition, technical policies and measures, including secure multi-party computing, trusted blockchain, labeling, Etc., should be adopted to ensure the transparency of data use, to address the concerns of the parties involved regarding the transfer of ownership or interest, and to protect the legitimate rights and interests of all parties involved.
- Promote the standardized development of the Big Data trading market, accelerate the construction of the credit investigation system, give full play to the role of the market mechanism in resource allocation, and improve the adequate circulation and efficient allocation of data.
- Strengthen the anti-monopoly regulation of data. Given the technical advantages and data-related capabilities of BigTech, licenses for transition to data services should be subject to strict regulation. In particular, the regulation of financial holding companies should be strengthened.
- Enhance the privacy protection of financial consumers. Policymakers and regulators should perfect the regulatory rules for the complete cycle management of personal data, covering data collection, data use, data transfer, and data deletion, Etc., strengthen the coordination among regulators, establish a joint prevention and control mechanism for privacy protection, and clarify the ethical boundaries for data application.
- Arise the self-protection awareness of financial consumers on the entire life cycle of their personal financial information.

In recent years, the financial regulators of major economies have gradually begun to strengthen their regulation and supervision of BigTech, through increasing penalties for conducting monopoly activities and inputting legislative efforts for data and

[12] LI W (2021) Improve data governance and strengthen privacy protection. Tsinghua Financial Review (1).

information protection and perfecting the regulatory framework for the FinTech industry, so as to prevent regulatory arbitrage and cross-border risk contagion at the legislative level.

In the past few years, the United States has launched a series of antitrust investigations against a number of BigTechs, including Facebook, Apple, Amazon, Etc. In addition, at the legislative level, in 2020, the California Consumer Privacy Act (the "CCPA") was enacted to strengthen privacy protection within California. In the same year, the Technology Lab of the Federal Deposit Insurance Corporation (the "FDIC") released Doing Business with Banks: Guidelines to Fintech Companies and Third-party Organizations, which requires FinTech companies and the relevant third-party companies to fully understand the legal and regulatory framework of the banking system and demonstrate their ability to continuously comply with applicable laws and regulations and establish appropriate monitoring systems for themselves.

From 2017 to 2019, the European Union fined Google amounting to roughly 8.25 billion euros for three consecutive years. In 2018, the EU implemented the General Data Protection Regulation (the "GDPR"), which aims to enhance individuals' control and rights over their personal data and simplify international business's regulatory environment. The GDPR is an essential component of EU privacy law and human rights law, in particular Article 8(1) of the Charter of Fundamental Rights of the European Union. In December 2020, the European Commission enacted the Digital Market Act (the "DMA"), passed by the European Legislature on 1 November 2022 and is to be formally implemented on 2 May 2023 with a six-month grace period. A dozen global digital platforms will be governed by the DMA by then, including Google, Apple, Facebook, Amazon, and Microsoft. Under the legislative purpose of making the markets in the digital sector fairer and more contestable, the DMA establishes a set of clearly defined objective criteria to identify "gatekeepers". Gatekeepers are large digital platforms providing so-called core platform services, such as online search engines, app stores, and messenger services. Gatekeepers must comply with the do's (i.e., obligations) and don'ts (i.e., prohibitions) listed in the DMA.[13]

China has also been trying to address the problems related to BigTech and the platform economy in recent years. For example, platform operators would be deemed as damaging fair market competition and impairing the legitimate rights and interests of financial consumers by Chinese regulators if forcing customers to "choose one from the other", conducting Big Data discrimination, and breaking the antitrust laws and regulations for failing to declare the implementation of business operator concentration, Etc.

The data issue over BitTech is closely related to antitrust legislation, investigation, and enforcement. In recent years, Chinese regulators have enacted several laws and regulations to address the platform economy's monopoly issue. The most representative one is the Anti-monopoly Guidelines of the Anti-monopoly Commission of the State Council on Platform Economy issued and effective on 7 February 2021. The Guidelines, by reference to the prominent competition problems of the platform economy that occurred in the past years, provide the basic principles, specific ideas,

[13] https://competition-policy.ec.europa.eu/dma_en.

and effective methods of antitrust regulation on the Internet platforms. For example, the Guidelines deem the requirement of "choose one from the other" and Big Data discrimination by Internet platforms as the abuse of dominant market position to limit market trading. Overall, the Guidelines respond to the necessity of antitrust efforts toward the platform economy.

Furthermore, for the effective regulation of BigTech, in 2020, the People's Bank of China (the "PBOC") formulated and implemented the Tentative Measures for Supervision and Administration of Financial Holding Companies in 2020. According to Article 6 of the Measures, Bigtechs with more than two types of financial licenses are required to apply for the establishment of a financial holding company.[14] The Measures impose prudential regulation on the financial activities conducted by FinTech companies and internet platforms. The Ant Group falls into Article 6 since it person has substantive control of five different types of financial institutions with certain business scales.

The PBOC has also been trying to prevent third-party payment institutions from occupying and misappropriating the customer reserves, which are under the unified custody of the PBOC. The PBOC also encourages third-party payment institutions to focus back on the payment business by stripping their clearing function to new financial infrastructures. At the end of 2020, the PBOC, the CBIRC, the CSRC and the State Administration of Foreign Exchange (the "SAFE"), four major financial regulators in China, jointly made an appointment with the Ant Group. The four

[14] According to Article 6 of the Tentative Measures for Supervision and Administration of Financial Holding Companies, a financial holding company should be established if a non-financial enterprise, natural person, or recognized legal person has substantive control over two or more different types of financial institutions and is under any of the following circumstances:

I. where the asset size of the financial institutions under substantial control that include commercial banks is no less than CNY500 billion, or where, although the asset size of the financial institutions is less than CNY500 billion, the asset size of the financial institutions other than commercial banks is no less than CNY100 billion, or the total scale of the assets entrusted for management is no less than CNY500 billion;

II. where asset size of the financial institutions under substantial control that does not include commercial banks is no less than CNY100 billion, or total assets under entrusted management is no less than CNY500 billion; and.

III. (III) where, although the asset size of the financial institutions under substantial control or the total scale of the assets entrusted for management fails to meet the standards set out in Items (I) and (II) above, the PBC considers it necessary to establish a financial holding company according to the macro-prudential regulation requirements.

For an enterprise group that satisfies the criteria stipulated in the preceding paragraph, if its financial assets constitute 85% or more of the group's total consolidated assets, the enterprise group may apply to establish a financial holding company specifically, and the financial holding company and its holding organizations should jointly constitute the financial holding group; or the parent company of the enterprise group may, pursuant to the same criteria for the establishment of a financial holding company stipulated herein, apply to become a financial holding company directly, the enterprise group will be deemed as a financial holding group entirely, and the ratio of financial assets to the group's total consolidated assets should continue to attain or exceed 85%.

regulators pointed out the problems of the Ant Group, which include the imperfect corporate governance mechanism, weak awareness of legal compliance, breaches of laws and regulations, regulatory arbitrage, abuse of market advantage to exclude competitors, and infringements of the rights and interests of consumers that result in consumer complaints. Afterward, the four regulators further raised a series of requirements to the Ant Group to rectify its key business areas. The requirements include the followings:

- Focus back on the payment business
- Improve transaction transparency
- Stop improper and illegal competitive behavior
- Keep licensed for carrying out financial business
- Legally conduct personal credit investigation business
- Pay attention to privacy protection
- Establish a financial holding company following the law, and strictly implement the regulatory requirements therein
- Ensure sufficiency of capital
- Comply with the laws and regulations regarding related transactions
- Improve corporate governance
- Rectify illegal financial conduct in the credit business, insurance business, and wealth management business, Etc.
- Ensure the legal compliance of the securities business, fund business, and asset securitization business
- Strengthen the governance of securities companies within the group.[15]

References

BIS (2019) Bigtech in finance: opportunities and risks. BIS Annual Economic Report

FSB (2020) BigTech firms in finance in emerging market and developing economies-market developments and potential financial stability implications. https://www.fsb.org/wp-content/uploads/P121020-1.pdf

Sun G (2017) Build a new ecology of financial technology, no 13. China Finance

[15] Pan G Vice governor of the people's bank of China, answered a reporter's question on the financial management department's interview with ant Group. http://www.pbc.gov.cn/goutongjiaoliu/113456/113469/4153479/index.html.

Chapter 4
Digital Currency

Introduction

Digital technology has iterated and developed rapidly in the past few years. If looking at the attributes of digital currency merely from the technical perspective, we might fall into the situation of "the blind feeling the elephant," where misunderstanding occurs due to lacking a comprehensive view. For a long while in the past, quite a few experts had believed that both distributed ledger databases and decentralized autonomous organization systems based on the consensus mechanism algorithms are necessary for the operation of Blockchain. This lopsided view led to a broad agreement that the stability of the value of the digital currency could only be ensured by decentralized technologies plus volume restriction over competent issuers of digital currencies.

However, this view was overruled by the occurrence and development of Bitcoin. The example that Libra abandons a certain degree of decentralization to improve transaction efficiency overturns the previous understanding believing that the digital currency should be based on decentralization. The misunderstanding is caused by the fact that these experts previously observed the digital currency merely from the technical perspective, without considering the historical and human factors in the course of currency evolution.

This book suggests that the discussion and study of Libra should not be limited to Libra itself but include the development trend of the digital currency embodied by the concept of Libra. For a comprehensive and accurate understanding of digital currency, in addition to the technical perspective, another two dimensions should be considered: the evolution of currency forms and the issuance of currency.

D. Zhao et al., *FinTech and SupTech in China*, Contributions to Finance and Accounting,
https://doi.org/10.1007/978-981-99-5173-4_4

4.1 Digital Currency from Evolution Perspective

Currency has evolved from physical currency to metal currency, paper money, and digital currency successively, corresponding to various forms of currencies, including commodity, gold & silver, paper, plastic card, and digital image. The trend of currency evolution is to increase user convenience and reduce production costs.

During early human society, things like shells were considered the major medium for commodities exchange due to their convenience to preserve and exchange. As time passed by, the mastery of metallurgy technology made metal currencies such as gold and silver regarded as the primary form of currency. The metal currency had played the role of currency for quite a long time, of its precious value and convenience for dividing and carrying. However, metal currencies also have several defects concerning circulation. For example,

- Bad currency drives out good currency
- The issuance volume is limited due to the objective restrictions from metal reserves and mining
- Inconvenience for long-distance carry requisite for big deals
- Economic problems like deflation could occur once the economic growth exceeds the supply of the metal currency.

With the economic scale enlarging, the accounting function of currency was highlighted while the currency's value was downplayed, leading to the occurrence of paper money. As early as the Song Dynasty, the paper money Jiaozi was born as a new currency form, using iron coins as collateral in exchange for notes for circulation. To some extent, Jiaozi can be regarded as the currency of the modern sense. Compared with metal currency, paper money has lower production costs and is more convenient to preserve, carry, and transport, avoiding the wear of coins in circulation. As such, paper money can be used in a broader range and adapted to a larger economic scale, which is conducive to the circulation of commodities and the advance of the commodity economy.

Some things could be improved in paper money. For example, it is accessible to counterfeit. However, the most deadly defect of paper money is its dependency on government capability, credit, and desire. For government desire, the government's random and unlimited issuance of paper money closely relates to hyperinflation, leading to an economic and social crisis.

With time moving to the digital era, when information technology is becoming mature and popular, the currency is technically allowed to show in digital images. The digital currency was born under this background. Digital currency payment is particularly advantageous for big deals, especially in the era of globalization, since electronic currency systems would make cross-border payments very convenient and low-cost.

In summary, the currency form evolves towards safety, convenience, and low cost.

- "Safety" means that a currency is hard to counterfeit, damage, and get impaired during circulation

- "Convenience" means that a currency is more convenient for payment and circulation, and the settlement efficiency thereof is higher
- "Low-cost" means that a currency cost has been decreased concerning its production, circulation, and exchange.

The above three outstanding advantages of digital currency make its value widely recognized. By now, digital currency can be regarded as the most advanced form in currency's progress. The value of the digital currency would not be affected by what kind of technical architecture it adopts, for example, whether decentralization is based, whether the Blockchain is applied, etc., just as the saying proposed by Xiaoping Deng at the start of China's reform and opening up, i.e., whether a cat is black or white, it is a good cat that catches mice.

4.2 Digital Currency from Issuance Perspective

From the evolution history of currency issuance, the currency has evolved from decentralization to centralization, from private to central bank issuance backed with state credit.

As a quasi-public good, modern currency is inseparable from state sovereignty. There are different types of currency, e.g., commodity currency and credit currency. Currencies also have many attributes in various aspects, e.g., natural attributes and social attributes.

The currency is more likely to be a private product from natural attributes and the early form. However, from its functions in the modern era, the currency should be regarded as a public or quasi-public product whose large-scale supply should be provided and managed by government or quasi-government institutions. For example, where a financial crisis caused by insufficient liquidity begins to occur, the central bank may provide liquidity to prevent the further spread of the such crisis.

Independent and reliable public or quasi-public institutions should support the socioeconomic function of a currency. Human society has transformed decentralization to centralization for currency issuance, from the issuance by private entities to issuance by the central bank under state credit. While decentralized issuance of currency by private entities cannot meet the needs of enlarging social and economic activities, the central bank issuance model can provide the currency with more safety and convenience and lower cost, which is proved to be a better path to play currency's role in promoting the economic efficiency.

The cost of information production and transmission makes it economically costly and operationally tricky for the public to grasp the credibility status of currency issuers. Government issuance can avoid such cost, whose public authority does not have to be proved by additional verifications. While the inherent authority of government replaces the need for information for reliability verifications, the transaction cost of such currency can be effectively reduced. Among various types of currencies, the most successful one is the one backup by reliable public issuers represented by the government. This ensures that the issued currencies are reliable, usable, value-stable, and widely accepted.

In most countries (China included), it is the central bank responsible for issuing currency. The central bank should have enough independence and government authority to ensure the reliability of and public trust in the issued currency. In this regard, although private cryptocurrencies may fulfill some of the functions of central bank currency, they still need to be viable alternatives. The historical trend and status of centralized issuance of currency (digital currency included) by central banks take much work to shake.[1]

4.3 The Nature and Function of Digital Currency

Along with the progress of information technology, digital currency is evolving and developing. Especially its monetary function is expanding, and its monetary attribute continues to strengthen. Early exploration of digital currency is mainly on electronic currencies, such as bank cards, bus cards, and network currencies (e.g., Tencent Q-coins), essentially electronic substitutes for physical cash and convertible to equivalent fiat currency. These electronic currencies mainly perform the payment function of a currency, which is usually subject to particular geographical and network community restrictions.

Both "electronic currency" and virtual "currency" are conceptually different from "digital currency." Moreover, the three are different in various aspects, including technical architecture, characteristics, and implementation scenarios.

Digital currency is constantly evolving, for example, from Bitcoin to Libra (Nakamoto 2008). During the process, digital currency's technical architecture and characteristics are also changing, with more monetary functions and more robust monetary attributes.

4.3.1 Community Cryptographic Digital Tokens Have Weak Monetary Attribute

"Community cryptographic digital token" refers to the digital currency endorsed by the community instead of state credit, whose issuance and circulation are closely related to and inseparable from the consensus rules of the community. Bitcoin is the first decentralized community cryptographic digital token, followed by a series of similar digital tokens. They may have minor differences concerning issuance manner, confirmation time, and used algorithm while naturally belonging to the same decentralized community cryptographic digital token category.

[1] Mersch (2019).

Decentralized community cryptographic digital token needs to be more robust as a medium of exchange. We will take Bitcoin as an example to explain this point hereunder. According to rough statistics, there are more than two thousand types of digital currencies, of which Bitcoin is the most successful and most broadly accepted, as you may be aware. Nonetheless, Bitcoin is rarely accepted as a medium of exchange due to its low efficiency. A simple Bitcoin transaction requires six miners for deal confirmation, while its mining rate usually stays at one dollar every ten minutes. It may take roughly an hour to complete a simple Bitcoin transaction. For more complex Bitcoin transactions, several hours may be taken.

Bitcoin needs to be stronger concerning value measurement and retention. Unlike traditional electronic money or paper money, Bitcoin neither represents the liability of an individual or institution nor is backed by government credit. The existence of paper money, which has no intrinsic value as broadly accepted statute currency, lies in the government credit behind it. The situation differs for Bitcoin since it needs more inherent value and government credit.

The value of Bitcoin is built based on a consensus that Bitcoin is "agreed" to be exchanged for other goods, services, or sovereign currencies. This consensus mechanism has led to the popularity of Bitcoin, whose price is volatile while traded and circulated. Example:

- The unit price of Bitcoin once was close to USD 20000 in January 2018 and continued to fluctuate significantly in the following months. However, with time moved, the unit price dived to USD 3,200 at the end of 2018 but recovered back to above USD 10000 again in June 2019.

Furthermore, since the number of algorithmic solutions is limited, the aggregated supply of Bitcoin in the market is also limited, making it unable to match the growing demands. While the little supply conflicts with the ever-increasing need, price fluctuations occur.

In summary, Bitcoin is weak with regard to the monetary function of a currency, and it is hard to act as a statutory currency. Classifying Bitcoin as an ordinary digital asset is more suitable than a currency.[2,3]

4.3.2 Digital Stablecoins Have Obvious Monetary Attribute

By nature, a stablecoin is a digital asset that is technically encrypted by Blockchain and whose value is stable compared with Bitcoin by its connection to valuable assets (e.g., sovereign currency). The tedcoin designed under the stablecoin concept was launched for the first time in the United States in 2015 since the issuance of stablecoin has become active around the globe. As of June 2019, 66 stablecoins were circulating in the market, while 134 stablecoin projects had been in the pipeline. Compared with

---

[2] Bank for International Settlements (2015).

[3] Berentsen and Schär (2018).

the community cryptographic digital currency that Bitcoin represents, stablecoin shows the more obvious monetary function and attribute mainly from the following aspects.

4.3.2.1 Convenient and Economical for Transaction Settlement

In order to address the transaction efficiency problem faced by Bitcoin, stablecoin gives up a certain degree of decentralization by improving and simplifying the programming language and consensus algorithm, etc., to speed up the settlement process of transactions.

Among various types of stablecoins, the most outstanding and unique advantage of Libra comes from the massive user base support from Facebook. By statistics, there are nearly 2.7 billion Facebook users globally. Given that the settlement significantly reduces the cost of cross-border payment settlement. However, given that the transaction settlement efficiency has been dramatically improved thanks to the popularity of electronic payment tools, the cost reduction room to be provided by stablecoin has been quite limited. China has walked so far in mobile payment that Chinese consumers have become accustomed to mobile technologies such as mobile banking, Alipay, WeChat, etc., which have already lowered the transaction cost and provided great convenience to a large extent. In Europe, the European Central Bank (the "ECB") launched the Target Instant Payment Settlement (the "TIPS") project to provide European consumers and enterprises with high-performance and 24-hour settlement solution. The ECB believes that TIPS is more secure and economical than traditional market-oriented retail payment innovations.

4.3.2.2 Capable for Value Measurement and Value Retention

Unlike Bitcoin, stablecoins can serve as modern currency since it has the function of value measurement and retaining as traditional currencies. Libra is similar to the Special Drawing Right (the "SDR"), consisting of a basket of fiat currencies whose issuance is backed by bank deposits and short-term government bonds. The "stable" of a stablecoin comes from its stable credit basis and stable value. So far, stablecoin has been widely leveraged to denominate certain commodities.[4]

4.3.3 Regulatory Concerns Around Digital Stablecoins

While producing economic and convenience value served as a currency, stablecoin has various potential risks that regulators should be cautious about. For example, although being a partially decentralized federation chain, Libra requires a certain

[4] Mersch (2019).

degree of decentralization to ensure its price stability. It is a false proposition for a centralized institution to issue decentralized stablecoins. For private currencies like Libra, there would be a moral hazard for issuers with regard to the overissue problem. From the perspective of stablecoins issuers, they do not profit from the interest they accrue for the stablecoin they issue but from the investment return with hard currency engaged. Tech giants may leverage their networks to exclude competitors and monetize information to exclusively access customers' personal and transaction data. New data protection, control, and ownership standards should be on regulators' agenda to address these potential issues.

There is a "fallacy of composition" phenomenon in the financial market, which is, even if the conduct is reasonable when taken by a single financial institution from a micro perspective, it might turn out to be unreasonable or even causes a systematic financial crisis when further taken by all or most financial institutions in the market. For example, using Libra might lead to the aforementioned "fallacy of composition." Individuals or enterprises may utilize Libra for settlement efficiency, payment safety, cost reduction, etc., which is reasonable from an individual angle. However, if most or all subjects in the market choose to develop and deploy stablecoins like Libra, the monetary and fiscal sovereignty of the country concerned might be impaired, or even worse, a systemic financial crisis could occur. Therefore, with respect to private crypto digital currency, relevant regulators should not only focus on micro advantages of private crypto digital currency, for example, security, efficiency, and cost reduction, but also pay attention to potential risks directly or indirectly related to financial market regulation in a macro level, to prevent the aforementioned "fallacy of composition" and avoid damage or danger to public interests.

In addition, for objective and comprehensive knowledge of private digital currencies, we should understand the significant regulatory risks and challenges caused by the widespread use of private digital currencies.

4.3.3.1 Impact the Fund Flow Management by Financial Regulators

Stablecoins have created a new channel of capital flow. The widespread of anonymous and peer-to-peer innovative transactions would speed up and complicate the cross-border flow of funds and therefore challenge financial regulators on fund flow monitoring and other relevant aspects. In China, the State Administration of Foreign Exchange (the "SAFE") manages the cross-border flow of funds. Suppose private digital currencies are widely adopted in commercial transactions in China. In that case, the SAFE might be heavily burdened with regard to CNY management, including foreign currencies denomination and foreign exchange management, etc.

Libra provides the users thereof with convenient cross-border payment and two-way convertibility with legal tenders. For example, a person may purchase Libra with USD and then exchange it for CNY through other dealers, challenging relevant regulators with regard to their management of foreign exchange and fund flow. Moreover, Libra payment is of anonymity and encryption, which, whilst helping to ensure transaction security, poses multiple potential market risks and regulatory challenges to regulators around the world with regard to Anti-Money Laundering ("the AML"), Counter-Terrorism Financing (the "CTF") and anti-tax evasion, etc.

In response, regulators should be able to regulate and supervise the decentralized value chain of stable-coin that involves wallet providers, crypto exchanges, verification nodes, investment vehicles, etc.

4.3.3.2 Impair the Monetary and Financial Sovereignty

As mentioned above, Libra is of anonymity, encryption, and unrestrained movement, complicating the regulatory task of monitoring the cross-border flow created thereby. Furthermore, the issuance of Libra can broadly impact the total volume of money creation within the monetary market and the social financing scale closely related to the borrowing and lending volume. In this respect, the broad issuance of private crypto digital currency would reduce the velocity of sovereign currencies and disorderly impact the monetary multiplier. When the transmission mechanism of monetary policy is distorted, a country's central bank or other competent regulators will find it hard to control the money supply effectively and ensure the monetary policy's effectiveness.

Such negative impacts could occur in any country or region where Libra can circulate freely. Moreover, when Libra is legally allowable to spread over the globe, the functions of sovereign currencies and the corresponding monitory policies could be heavily weakened, especially in the countries or regions with the high inflation rate and imperfect financial systems, since people in these areas would be likely to abandon the local currency and turn to the stable-coin which is backed by other robust and stable foreign currencies. Therefore, small economies should especially consider whether their local currencies would be replaced if private digital currencies flow freely on their lands. If so, issuing private digital currencies could be another form of dollarization, undermining the local monetary policy, financial development, and economic growth.

China is making efforts for the internationalization of CNY, which could be affected by the comprehensive issuance of Libra if the CNY is not included in the basket of underlying currencies. The problem is that the said basket is decided by a private entity, i.e., Facebook, lacking international recognition, which is necessary since, as mentioned above, the sovereignty and internationalization degree of a statutory currency could be affected.

4.3.3.3 Replace Partial Fiscal Sovereignty

A country's central bank (or a similar organ) is responsible for representing the taxpayers in capturing the profits generated from the gap between the face value and the production cost of a statutory currency.

If Libra wholly or partially replaces the statutory currency in a country, the country's government would lose part or all of the power to produce and manage the currency. In other words, the government would need help to collect the seigniorage, which would significantly reduce the government revenue. Moreover, the income is closely related to the ability of a government to monetize fiscal deficits, which would impair the financing capacity and increase the risk of the government bond default at the market level.

4.3.3.4 Disorder the Monetary and Fiscal Policies

The European sovereign debt crisis started on December 8, 2009, and produced multiple adverse outcomes for the economy of Europe in the following years. This long-term crisis has shown us the importance of consistency and coordination between monetary and fiscal policies. Otherwise, there would be a high likelihood of a financial or debt crisis outbreak.

Suppose a country expects the sovereign currency issued thereby to become a globally accepted currency. In that case, the government should cede the monetary and fiscal sovereignty and maintain the power to keep harmonizing the monetary policy and fiscal policy within the country, which might be under significant threat shortly.

As provided in the 2019 joint statement by G20 finance ministers and central bank governors, among others, crypto assets lack specific critical attributes of sovereign currencies and might affect the financial stability of a country if widely issued and circulated as currencies. Thus, for the sake of monetary and fiscal sovereignty and financial stability, and the prevention of systemic crises, countries or regions cannot be too cautious in allowing Libra or other similar digital currencies to legally issue and circulate on their territory, let alone the complete replacement of original statutory currencies.

4.3.4 Strengthen the Regulation of Private Crypto Digital Currencies

International organizations and countries may have different attitudes towards crypto assets, such as digital currencies. For example, in China, India, and Indonesia, the regulators prohibit private crypto digital currencies. On the other hand, in the United States, the United Kingdom, France, Australia, and Japan, private crypto digital currencies are strictly regulated by regulators. In many other countries, regulators are open to or impose prudent regulation over private crypto digital currencies. However, the overall regulatory environment around the globe tends to be increasingly stricter since, at early stages, central banks or other competent financial regulators did not treat private digital tokens as "currencies" considering the rapid price fluctuations (Wang 2018a).

In the United States, private crypto digital currencies were classified as financial assets in the early days when they were circulated and used only on a limited scale and had no substantial impact on financial stability and monetary and fiscal policies. However, things have become different since the issuance of Libra, which is backed by Facebook's extensive internet network and global user base. And the situation could be the same or similar for many other similar stablecoins, which, once launched, would spread and proliferate at an alarming speed and further affect substantially the Anti-Money Laundering (the "AML") regulation, Counter-Terrorism Financing (the "CTF") regulation, and the stability of the financial market.

As a result, many countries worldwide have begun to be more cautious about launches of private crypto digital currencies represented by Libra. As a result, they may formulate and implement measures and actions, including access restrictions, circulation scope restrictions, and stricter regular regulation and supervision.

For example, in recent years, the United States and the United Kingdom have strengthened risk management over private crypto financial assets. For example, the Securities and Exchange Commission of the United States issued a risk alert in early 2020, stating that the Initial Exchange Offerings (the "IEOs") are inconsistent with the securities laws and regulations and reminding investors to be wary of such activities that use new technical concepts to make false promises of high returns. In the United Kingdom, the Financial Conduct Authority (the "FCA") also announced in January 2020 that the activities concerning private crypto assets should be subject to AML and CTF regulation and supervision. In addition, it imposed registration requirements for all crypto asset trading and wallet service providers.

The International Organization of Securities Commissions (the "IOSCO") produced a research report entitled "Global Currency Stability Plan" in March 2020, stating that stablecoins around the globe should be subject to securities market regulatory frameworks. For a stablecoin to be a globally recognized digital currency, government support as well as strict regulation matter. It has been argued that while Libra's success could be better, its idea of aiming at a basket of currencies represents a possible trend toward globalized currencies in the future.[5,6,7]

---

[5] Chantilly (2019).

[6] Yuan and Wang (2020).

[7] On July 9, 2019, at the seminar of "Reform and Development of Foreign Exchange Administration in China," Zhou X, president of China Society for Finance and Banking, gave his views on the issuance of Libra on the future development of currency under the situation of globalization.

4.4 Digital Currencies Issued by Governmental Authorities

4.4.1 Background

Even a relatively mature stablecoin like Libra could find it challenging to become a truly global currency, given the strict regulatory environment. Therefore, it might not become a future protagonist of the international monetary system. Nevertheless, Libra could catalyze monetary change, forcing monetary authorities and regulators to choose between central-bank-managed digital currencies and riskier private digital tokens. At the heart of this trade-off is a system of financial inclusion that provides residents suffering from financial repression with more financial choices. However, at the cost of lower government revenues, potentially more volatile capital flows, and even systemic risk.

But the choice tends to favor the latter because central banks have a strong interest in maintaining control over the payments system and the broader financial sector, safeguarding the attractiveness of their currencies, and a stronger sense of responsibility for guarding against systemic risk. So far, major national and regional central banks have embraced technical developments in the currency area and are actively exploring the issuance of Central Bank Digital Currency (the "CBDC"), which has multiple advantages over digital currencies issued by the private sector.

4.4.1.1 Regulation Facilitation

When directly involved in providing digital currencies, central banks and other competent financial regulators would be more convenient to guarantee consumer protection, privacy standards, and payment compliance. In principle, private currency issuers like Libra could be subject to the same regulation and monitoring. But, as experience shows, this is not easy when the interests are completely misaligned.

4.4.1.2 Serve for Macroeconomic Regulation

If issued by the central banks or other competent financial regulators responsible for macroeconomic regulation and financial stability, digital currencies can assist these authorities in managing the macroeconomic and relevant international implications of digital currencies.

At the very least, central banks can always ensure that the swaps of CBDC deposits will not have any negative macroeconomic consequences.

4.4.1.3 Promote Financial Inclusion

The CBDC could improve efficiency, reduce the cost of payments, and promote financial inclusion. Cash management could be quite costly for some countries and regions, with geography as the primary cause. Poor populations in unbanked areas might have no or limited access to formal payment systems, and the CBDC is able to address the financial needs of these populations based on the digitalization and safety thereof, which will enlarge the coverage of formal financial services and ultimately promote the financial inclusion level, through mobile clients and network communications.

Besides, the CBDC can reduce costs and improve efficiency as well. At the retail level, the CBDC is generally efficient and convenient in acting as an effective supplement to cash, which is helpful to complement existing electronic payment instruments and enhance competition in the payment market.

The CBDC, if it provides interest to its holders, would have a saving function and be an alternative to existing electronic payment instruments, which are less secure. Moreover, if issued by batch, the CBDC would help improve the large-value settlement, enhance the efficiency and security of cross-border payments, reduce the cost of payments, and facilitate international trade and financial transactions.

4.4.1.4 Stable in Payment and Friendly to Start-ups

The payment function of the CBDC is stable regarding operation and maintenance. Besides, compared with private cryptocurrencies, the CBDC provides lower thresholds and remains relatively friendly to start-ups. In some countries, for example, Sweden and China, there is an increasing concentration of payment systems in the hands of large companies. In response, some central banks seek to issue their digital currencies to enhance the flexibility of their payment systems and enhance competition in the sector.[8]

4.4.2 Global Developments of the CBDC

Apart from the PBOC, many other central banks around the globe have also launched a series of research and projects for the issuance preparation of the CBDC. According to a survey of central banks of 21 advanced economies and 44 developing economies by the Bank for International Settlements (the "BIS") in the fourth quarter of 2020, the share of central banks actively working on CBDCs has grown by about one-third to 86% over the past four years. Central banks mainly focus on retail CBDCs, with inclusive finance and enhanced payments as the main drivers. According to the survey, central banks surveyed are moving from the proof-of-concept stage to the

[8] Zhang (2020).

experimental stage, with about 60% (42% in 2019) conducting proof-of-concept or experiments and 14% moving forward with pilot arrangements.

Quite a few central banks have begun to pilot the CBDC recently. For example, to follow the trend for non-cash payments and reduce the cost of issuing banknotes, Riksbank, the Swedish central bank, launched the R&D of e-krona in 2017 and initiated a pilot program in February 2020. Moreover, the use of cash in Sweden has declined sharply in the past decade, prompting the Riksbank to follow up on the CBDC. As a result, e-krona is positioned as a complementary tool to cash and belongs to the retail CBDC in the category. According to the CBDC classification, E-krona is interest-free, adopts a two-tier operation model, uses distributed accounting technology, and follows limited anonymity. In addition, the central banks of China, Uruguay, Ukraine, Cambodia, the Bahamas, and other countries have also carried out CBDC pilots.

Central banks in some economies are developing and experimenting with CBDCs. For example, the Bank of Japan and the European Central Bank, in order to improve the efficiency of large cross-border payments and securities settlement systems, proposed and jointly developed a wholesale CBDCs (Stella project) in 2016 and implemented tests on interbank settlement, delivery versus payment settlement, simultaneous settlement, balancing confidentiality and audibility in the economy, etc., and achieved the expected objectives. Furthermore, in December 2019, the European Central Bank published a report on the retail CBDCs (EURO chain project), which is positioned as an alternative to cash, adopts a two-tier operating model, follows limited anonymity, and is still under constant development and perfection.

In July 2020, the Bank of Japan (the "BOJ") published a technical report on the penetration and operational resilience of the CBDC. In such a report, the BOJ claimed to explore the feasibility of the CBDC through empirical trials.

In the United Kingdom, the Bank of England (the "BOE") proposed the RS Coin project in 2015 to study the CBDC in collaboration with the University College London (the "UCL"). The BOE and UCL have carried out some small-scale experiments in the project. RS Coin belongs to retail CBDC and adopts a hybrid architecture combining centralized and distributed accounting and a two-tier operating mode. In March 2020, the BOE systematically explained the design ideas of retail CBDC and presented the vision of the future CBDC from multiple dimensions, such as issuance objectives, design principles, operation models, system application technologies, etc. As provided by the BOE, the CBDC is expected to be an innovation of currency form and related payment infrastructures. The private sector could be engaged to supplement the cash and help the BOE achieve its policy objectives.

Central banks in some economies are trying to demonstrate the feasibility of the CBDC. However, they have no specific plans for R&D. In the United States, the Federal Reserve is conducting an assessment of the cost and benefit of the CBDC, as well as research and experiments on distributed accounting technologies and potential uses thereof in the field of digital currencies. Australia, India, Italy, Norway, Denmark, and other countries are also actively researching the CBDC.[9]

---

[9] PBOC (2020).

4.4.3 e-CNY Designed by the PBOC

The People's Bank of China (the "PBOC"), as the central bank of China, has put forward and promoted Chinese CBDC (e-CNY) in recent years in order to adapt to the digital economy, address the decline of cash use volume, boost the competition in the payment market, ensure the payment security for the public, improve the efficiency of payment business and promote the financial inclusion. The PBOC has carried out a series of studies of digital fiat currency as early as 2014. In 2016, the PBOC established its Digital Currency Research Institute (DCRI), a financial infrastructure designed to advance the development of e-CNY. In 2018, the PBOC formulated an e-CNY R&D framework, providing basic guidelines for R&D. In July 2021, the Working Group on e-CNY Research and Development under the PBOC published a white paper titled Progress of Research and Development of E-CNY in China, which systematically disclosed the ideas behind the top-level design for the first time. Specifically, e-CNY adopts a two-tier operation: the central bank performs centralized management to regulate currency issuance and implement monetary policies; commercial institutions make the best of their advantages in resources, talents and technologies to disperse risks and avoid financial disintermediation through a market-driven system that promotes competition (Fan 2018).

While advancing the pilot program on e-CNY R&D and application, the PBOC has made continuous efforts to improve institutional arrangements so as to strengthen personal information protection. Complying with the Cybersecurity Law, the Personal Information Protection Law, the Anti-Money Laundering Law, and other laws and regulations, e-CNY puts in place a number of institutional arrangements and employs various technical tools to ensure personal information security and prevent potential violations and crimes.

The key design points of the CBDC by the PBOC include the quantity design, hierarchy design, preparation system, and pricing mechanism. In addition, the choice of issuance mode of the CBDC could affect how the CBDC would participate in economic activities, what outcomes would be for various financial elements and other participants of economic activities, the capacity of the central bank to perform its duties, and the transmission path of the monetary policy. These aspects are in intimate relation to the overall framework of the future monetary system and would be fundamental considerations for designing a CBDC system (Wang 2018b).

4.4.3.1 Account-Based CBDC Versus Token-Based CBDC

One of the most important ways to classify CBDCs based on whether they are account-based or token-based. The account-based CBDC settles transactions via digital currency accounts opened with a central bank or one or more commercial banks. The token-based CBDC settles transactions by tokens in digital wallets via a centralized or decentralized settlement system.

4.4.3.2 Single-Issuer CBDC Versus Multi-Issuer CBDC

Another important way to classify CBDCs based on their issuing mode. For example, the CBDC could be designed as a single-issuer CBDC or multi-issuer CBDC. To outward seeming, the CBDC is classified based on the number of issuers and managing bodies. To inward seeming, the core of this classification is whether different digital currencies are allowed to coexist under one digital currency framework.

Our latest research shows that most CBDCs are uniquely issued and endorsed by one central bank, whilst a few are collectively issued and endorsed by multiple. The multi-issuer CBDC would connect with other CBDCs and may even have a connection and unified operation with private digital currencies.

4.4.3.3 Single-Tier CBDC Versus Multi-tier CBDC

This is to classify CBDCs based on their operation modes. So far, there are two major operation modes of fiat digital currencies. The first mode is single-tier operation, in which a central bank issues the CBDC directly to the public. The second mode is a two-tier operation, in which a central bank indirectly issues the CBDC through traditional commercial banks to the public, similar to the conventional "central bank—commercial banks" currency issuance dual mode. In the latter, there will be a central bank to exchange the CBDCs with commercial banks and other institutions first, and they will subsequently exchange the CBDCs with the public.

4.4.3.4 Interest-Bearing CBDC Versus Interest-Free CBDC

This is to classify the CBDC based on whether the CBDC provides interests for its holders. The issue of whether the CBDC should bear interest will have potential impacts on the economy and the financial market. Therefore, this issue is one of the most important topics of recent CBDC research.

One view is that if used merely as a payment instrument rather than an interest-bearing asset, the CBDC will be equivalent to variants of traditional payment instruments. Its role is more like the digitization of cash. At present, the interest-free mode is adopted by a majority.

Another view advocates that the CBDC should be interest-bearing, from which the CBDC could have a value retention function with a rate of return comparable to other risk-free assets such as short-term government securities or central bank reserves. In the theoretical studies on the impact of CBDCs on social welfare, economic growth, and financial markets, most CBDCs are set as interest-bearing.

4.4.3.5 Non-anonymous CBDC Versus Anonymous CBDC

This is to classify the CBDC based on anonymity. Central banks have to face whether to issue digital currency anonymously, to what extent, and how to balance anonymity and other aspects, including privacy protection, security, risk management, etc.

Notwithstanding the preceding, most of the CBDCs play as a substitute for cash. Before issuing the CBDC, the central bank must fully consider in advance the issues in relation to AML, CTF, anti-tax evasion, and other regulatory areas. The design of CBDC requires a certain degree of anonymity, which may differ for different roles involved in CBDC circulation, including trading parties, third parties, governments, and regulators. It should be consistent with relevant regulatory policies.

4.4.3.6 Pilot Application and Scenarios Development[10]

Up till now, the PBOC has carried out pilot e-CNY application in selected areas in 15 provinces and municipalities and designated 10 operators based on a comprehensive evaluation. Top-level designs, including the two-tier operational system, have passed all-round tests, and their feasibility and reliability have been verified. An open e-CNY ecology and competition mechanism have effectively mobilized market entities and created a sound environment for fair competition.

A wide array of online and offline e-CNY application models have been built in wholesale, retail, catering, culture, tourism, education, healthcare, and public services, which can be replicated and applied in other areas. As of August 31, 2022, the pilot areas in 15 provinces and municipalities have recorded 360 million e-CNY transactions with a total value of RMB100.04 billion, and over 5.6 million stores have accepted payment in e-CNY. Since the beginning of 2022, governments of the pilot areas have launched nearly 30 e-CNY "red packets" campaigns themed "promoting consumption," "fighting the COVID-19," "advocating low-carbon travel," etc. In addition, commercial institutions have launched multiple market-oriented promotional campaigns. All these have effectively recovered consumption in society and unleashed consumption potential. During the 2022 Beijing Winter Olympics and Paralympics, e-CNY, as a significant achievement of China's fintech development, was further promoted, satisfying the mobile payment needs of spectators in sports venues and offering a safe and efficient innovative payment method for overseas visitors to China. The Tanpuhui (Inclusive Carbon Emissions Reduction) platform and green riding activities use e-CNY for transaction settlements, providing new ways to implement the "dual carbon" strategy. Many local governments have introduced e-CNY payment services in their e-government service platforms, enabling online and offline payments to public utilities, and they have used e-CNY to hand out tax refunds, special funds for monthly medical insurance settlement, aid funds for residents in need, and support funds for enterprises with specialized skills, sophisticated

[10] http://www.pbc.gov.cn/en/3688006/4671762/4688130/index.html.

operation, unique products, and innovative abilities. In addition, the coverage of e-CNY services has been expanded to incorporate counties and villages to promote rural financial services based on distinctive application scenarios such as agricultural product sales and preferential agricultural subsidies, in a bid to support rural revitalization and the building of digital villages.

4.4.3.7 The PBOC Has Continuously Advanced Product R&D and Service Upgrading[11]

The PBOC has strengthened the supply of basic products. It has developed the "e-CNY" APP to provide easy currency exchange, payment, and wallet management, among other services, and support online and offline e-CNY applications in all scenarios. It has launched multiple forms of hardware wallets, explored the possibility to integrate software and hardware in products, and developed functions to accommodate extreme scenarios where there is no access to network or electricity. In addition, leveraging the high efficiency and low cost of e-CNY, the PBOC has introduced differentiated corporate payment and settlement schemes to serve the real economy.

Exploring the application of smart products. As the digital version of fiat currency, e-CNY boasts the advantages of trust, connectivity and second-mover in establishing an ecosystem supporting the application of smart contracts, which is conducive to increasing the transparency of transactions, improving the intelligence of capital management, and reducing the costs of settlement and compliance. At present, e-CNY smart contracts have been applied in government subsidies, retail marketing, and prepayment management.

Improving accessible and senior-friendly designs. Focusing on capacity building of accessible services and bridging the digital divide, the PBC has been advancing e-CNY R&D in line with the requirements of both financial inclusion and a people-driven e-CNY product system. As such, it incorporated accessibility into the overall planning at the beginning of product design. Based on the features of e-CNY, the PBOC has put forward the inclusive design concept of "controlling the source, building a system, ensuring scalability, and bringing warmth," and made both software and hardware products more adaptive (Fan 2016).

4.4.3.8 Conclusion

For CBDC issuance and circulation, a central bank should consider the policy background in advance. For example, suppose the policy objective is to develop a new statutory electronic payment instrument. In that case, the CBDC should be designed as interest-free, convertible against statutory currencies in equivalency, collateralized with deposit reserves, etc. On the other hand, if the policy objective is to form a new

[11] http://www.pbc.gov.cn/en/3688006/4671762/4688130/index.html.

monetary policy instrument, the CBDC should be designed as interest-bearing and collateralized with treasury bonds or other high-grade bonds.

The impact of the CBDC on the financial system is intimately related to its fundamental design ideas. Generally speaking, a CBDC designed as a monolayer operation, interest-bearing, value-based (based on Blockchain), and collateralized with treasury bonds tends to significantly impact the financial system. Whether to adopt Blockchain in CBDC design should be subject to comprehensive and objective analysis. Blockchain has the benefits of decentralization and non-tamperability. However, decentralization may not be the core of the modernization of the payment system, as the possibility of tampering with the current financial institution account system could be higher. On the other side, Blockchain may also raise many new questions and regulatory challenges to payment, such as how to make modifications in case of transaction errors.

Under careful consideration of the CBDC's impact on monetary policy, deposits, market liquidity, etc., the design of a country's CBDC should also be considered from easy to complex. A CBDC, if designed as a dual-level operation and interest-free, supporting flexible implementation and having characteristics of electronic payment instruments, would better serve the financial market. The above design idea can minimize CBDC's negative impact on the market, prevent and defuse financial risks, serve the real economy, and optimize payment ecology (Wang 2016).

References

Bank for International Settlements (2015) Digital currencies, report of the committee of payments and market infrastructures

Berentsen A, Schär F (2018) A short introduction to the world of cryptocurrencies. Federal Reserve Bank of St. Louis Review, First Quarter

Chantilly (July 2019) Chair's summary: G7 finance ministers and central bank governors' meeting. https://www.bis.org/publ/arpdf/ar2019e3.pdf

Fan Y (2016) The theoretical basis and architecture choice of China's legal digital currency. China Finance (11)

Fan Y (2018) Some thoughts on central bank digital currency. First Financial Daily

Mersch Y (2019) Member of the executive board of the European central bank. In: Money and private currencies—reflections on libra, speech at the ESCB Legal conference. Frankfurt am Main

Nakamoto S (2008) Bitcoin: a peer-to-peer electronic cash system, https://bitcoin.org/bitcoin.pdf

PBOC (Nov 2020) China Financial Stability Report. China Financial Publishing House.

Wang X (2018a) Strengthen the supervision of virtual currency and firmly safeguard the right to issue national currency. First Finance, Issue 4

Wang X (2018b) Why should we study the issuance of central bank digital currency. Caixin Weekly, Issue 9

Wang X, Ren Z (2016) Digital currency and its regulatory response. China Finance, Issue 17

Yuan J, Wang Q (2020) Multi-dimensional view of the development trend of digital currency. Banker, Issue 1

Zhang T (2020) Advantages and challenges of central bank digital currency. Tsinghua Financ Rev 8

Chapter 5
Financial Consumer Protection in Fintech Field

Introduction

With the full integration of science and finance, modern information technologies, such as the Internet, Big Data, Cloud Computing, AI, and Blockchain, have been widely applied to the financial sector, and "technology plus" has injected a new driving force to achieve leapfrog development in finance. With the rapid growth and popularization of Internet technology and mobile terminals, financial services have gradually migrated from offline to online services and have comprehensively ushered in the Internet era. Financial institutions may construct or rent cloud platforms to establish core systems and complete the leap of infrastructure to the "cloud," which will not only enable them to carry increasingly complex business scenarios but also provide technical solutions to cope with high concurrent situations effectively, develop new financial consumption scenarios, improve operating efficiency and control operating costs. By using Big Data technology, financial institutions can map an "accurate portrait" of customers, which provides the possibility for precision marketing, improving their risk control ability, enriching consumption scenarios, and enhancing the loyalty of consumers. The development and application of AI technology can transform credit management, risk control, marketing, customer service, and debt collection processes, thus promoting the financial sector to enter an "intelligence era. " Blockchain technology, as a distributed accounting technology, has characteristics such as information transparency, difficulty in tampering, anonymity, intelligent execution, etc., that have made it possible to alleviate the "pain points" in protecting financial consumers (Yang 2015).

However, it should be considered that while improving the quality and efficiency of financial services comprehensively, science has also brought new risks and challenges to protecting financial consumers' rights and interests. For example, with the increasing complexity of "technology + finance" products, financial consumers' insufficient financial and technological knowledge, the problem of excessive debt brought about by the improved availability of financial services has gradually become prominent. Furthermore, in the open Internet environment, financial consumers'

D. Zhao et al., *FinTech and SupTech in China*, Contributions to Finance and Accounting,
https://doi.org/10.1007/978-981-99-5173-4_5

data and information are always at risk of leakage; some platforms have formed "monopoly advantages" under "technology advantages" and "flow advantages," and the rights and interests of financial consumers are often infringed upon. Given this, to boost the transformation and upgrading of financial services, it is of high theoretical value and practical significance to study how to comprehensively strengthen the protection of financial consumers based on encouraging and supporting technological innovation (EC 2018).

5.1 Critical Problems Facing Financial Consumer Protection at Present

Although the application of technology in the financial sector is beneficial to promoting the development of financial inclusion, it also brings a series of new risks and problems, resulting in frequent infringements upon the rights and interests of financial consumers and posing new challenges to the protection of financial consumers.

5.1.1 The Dilemma of "Double Gaps"

In the Fintech era, Internet consumer finance has been deeply integrated with science, and such integration is in all fields and processes. However, compared with the high speed of technology iteration and product iteration in Internet consumer finance, financial consumers often lack sufficient financial expertise and understanding with regard to the mechanisms of how technology is operated and applied and their overall level of financial literacy and technology literacy is not high. For example, technology has made certain Internet consumer finance products more accessible, enabling more consumers to enjoy the benefits of "technology + finance" more conveniently and at a lower cost. Nevertheless, these products not only have financial attributes but are also endowed with technological attributes, so their business complexity has increased rather than decreased, which places higher and more requirements for financial and technical knowledge levels of financial consumers. Besides, in the open Internet environment, financial consumers' personal information and behavioral data are exposed to greater risk of leakage, so how to enhance the sensitivity of financial data and awareness of privacy protection has become an essential topic for protecting financial consumers. In addition, some criminals may use counterfeit Apps and phishing websites to commit actual fraud on consumers in the name of financial innovation, which also requires financial consumers to improve their ability to distinguish pseudo-financial technologies continuously. Only through constantly improving financial consumers' financial and technological literacy can we narrow the gap between finance and technology and make financial consumers thoroughly enjoy the bonus of "technology + finance".[1]

5.1.2 *Excessive Debt*

From the perspective of service targets, Internet consumer finance platforms have penetrated the group with low education backgrounds and low income. According to the 47th Statistical Report on China's Internet Development,[2] by December 2020, the number of netizens with a junior college degree or below has reached 90.7%, and the number of netizens with a monthly income of less than 3,000 yuan has gained 51.1%. According to the 2020 Report on the Development of China Consumer Finance Companies[3] Issued by the China Banking Association, in the survey, 11 consumer finance companies reported that although the proportion of customers with a monthly income of less than 3,000 yuan was less than 25%, it was increasing; 4 consumer finance companies reported that the balance of the customers with a monthly income of less than 3,000 yuan exceeded 50%, highlighting the prominent feature of providing services to the low-income groups. However, due to income instability, once the low-income groups cannot afford to repay the loans, they are likely to fall into the trouble of "borrowing new loans to repay old loans."

Excessive marketing of Internet consumer finance products produces induction. In the environment of increasingly advanced consumption scenario, e-commerce platforms can accurately analyze the characteristics of users' financial behaviors based on data mining technology, push a large number of financial marketing advertisements and attractive products to users, and then provide various "installment interest-free, and fee-free" financial products in the payment link, creating a great temptation for the vulnerable people, leading to the prevalence of premature consumption and excessive consumption, and eventually leaving consumers with heavy debts. For example, a survey of college students showed that 45% of the respondents in Hangzhou often use Ant Credit Pay, 25% undergo excessive consumption, and 20% experience overdue repayment. It is worth noting that the high cost of borrowing will lead to financial disfavor. For example, a single loan is from 1000 to 10000 yuan and can be repaid in installments of 10–24 years, with an annual interest rate of 21% and an annual customer service fee of 14.57%. This means that the combined yearly interest rate is close to 36%. For some other credit products, the nominal interest rate is lower than 36%, but the interest rate may reach 70–80% if calculated based on compound interest. If additional loan service and consulting fees are added, the overall interest rate may exceed 100%.

---

[1] (Dongrong 2020).

[2] China Internet Network Information Center (Jul 2021) Statistical Report on China's Internet Development.

[3] China Banking Association (Aug 2020) Development Report on Chinese Consumer Finance Companies.

Some financial intermediaries outside the scope of financial regulation lure financial consumers to get loans through Internet channels with the wordings such as "low interest, low fee, fast, no guarantee, and no credit review," making it very easy for such financial consumers to fall into a "loan trap (Ye 2015)."

5.1.3 Coexistence of Excessive Information Collection and Data Leakage

Some Internet consumer finance platforms excessively collect and use user data. According to the regulatory requirements, consumer financial companies should follow the principle of minimization of the information collection when carrying out business. However, the platforms usually take their market advantages, in which consumers must upload not only their personal identity information and biometric characteristics but also their consumption and payment data, and even the personal database will be needed to be accessed with authorization. In February 2021, the Communications Administration of Guangdong Province notified 12 financial Apps of infringement upon users' rights and interests, in which 9 of them failed to specify the purpose, method, and scope of personal information collection and use by the third-party SDK integrated with the Apps. In addition, it is common for users to agree to the privacy policy by default at the time of registration and login or apply for terminal permission in advance without having read and agreed to the privacy policy. After obtaining a large amount of unauthorized data from users, consumer financial institutions often process the data, analyze the social attributes, living habits, consumption bias, etc., of users, and then make profits through targeted push advertising, products, promotions, etc.

At present, consumer financial companies master not only various financial and non-financial information of consumers but also behavioral data of consumers such as consumption habits, payment preferences, social networks, etc. Therefore, improper storage or cyber-attacks may lead to privacy leakage, significant property losses, and personal safety risks. In addition, with data elements being increasingly important, some platforms may have illegal acts or irregularities of "packaging" the personal information and behavioral data of financial consumers for sale. For example, in December 2020, the China Consumer News Agency and the China Digital 100 Data Academy jointly issued the Survey Report on Consumer Credit Behaviors and Financial Consumer Rights Protection Awareness, which showed that 29.2% of the respondents had encountered infringements, most of which are suspected personal information leakage (accounting for 55.2%) (Li 2021).

5.1.4 Technology Defects Decrease User Experience

Financial consumers will likely be entrenched and stratified, resulting in consumer discrimination. Internet consumer financial platforms use Big Data technology to generate "portraits" based on the economic, social networking, consumption habits, and other information it holds on financial consumers and recommends complementary products, services, and pricing accordingly.

However, as the data collection dimensions and core algorithms are convergent when all platforms use the same or similar carving tools, some vulnerable groups will have no access to financial services or can not receive the best quality services all the time, failing to "universalize" finance.

Some technologies that have yet to be well-verified are hastily put into use, and their fatal technical defects and algorithmic loopholes will give rise to systemic risks.

5.1.5 Hidden Dangers of Oligopoly and Unfair Competition

Technologies can help improve Internet consumer financial platforms' service efficiency and quality. However, we still need to guard against the excessive use of financial technologies, which may lead to market monopolies and unfair competition among some large technology companies, which may, thereby,

- "Level up" financial consumers through algorithms and conduct Big Data discrimination, which may, among others, prevent sticky and less price-sensitive consumers from preferential services.
- Monopolize access to data and obstruct fair competition.
- Increase financial consumers' dependencies and switching costs (The Research Group of the Financial Consumer Protection Bureau of the People's Bank of China 2021).

5.2 Policy Suggestions for Comprehensive Financial Consumer Protection

5.2.1 Improve Financial Literacy of Financial Consumer

First, financial authorities and financial institutions should use a variety of education carriers and design a variety of scenarios, to carry out financial and technological education for financial consumers anytime and anywhere. Financial regulators and financial institutions should create a fixed, convenient, and suitable channel for financial consumers through online and offline education, push the latest financial and technological knowledge to financial consumers, and bridge the "knowledge gap" of financial consumers to the greatest extent.

Second, financial authorities should take the lead in carrying out targeted financial and technological literacy education activities regularly or irregularly, combining with themes such as FinTech. Financial consumers can have their financial questions answered through the "face-to-face" introductions and explanations in the activities and establish a scientific, financial consumption concept.

Third, attention to and education of critical groups of people should also be strengthened. It is necessary for financial authorities and financial institutions to jointly carry out the "Financial Knowledge Entering Campus" activity with education departments, strengthen the financial education of students and guide student groups to establish the concept of rational consumption through broadcasting short videos on financial knowledge, posting posters, printing and distributing financial knowledge manuals, carrying out classroom games, etc. Meanwhile, by explaining typical cases, students should be informed to recognize and prevent illegal loans, such as campus loans and loan traps, etc., to enhance their self-protection ability. At the same time, financial authorities and financial institutions should also jointly work with local communities to organize the "Financial Knowledge Community" activity to keep the elderly promptly informed of the supportive policies, reforming measures. Current developments in the financial field through the printing and distribution of manuals and posters, etc., helping them establish a rational investment concept, deepening their understanding of the risks and benefits of financial products, preventing various new types of financial frauds, and avoiding them falling into "financial traps".[4]

5.2.2 Explore Classification and Grading of Financial Consumer

Internet consumer finance platforms should be actively promoted to use Big Data technologies to classify and grade financial consumers, achieve precise marketing and reasonable pushing, and protect their rights and interests from being infringed to the maximum extent. Internet consumer finance platforms may, by virtue of Big Data technologies, assess the risk tolerance of financial consumers and push lending products suitable for financial consumers' risk tolerance based on their educational background, occupation information, personal or household income, investment experience, debts, and differences in risk tolerance. For financial consumers with solid risk tolerance, stable income, good credit, and strong lending experience, their lending limit may be appropriately increased and lending interest rates reduced; for financial consumers with poor risk tolerance, unstable income, or even lack of source of income, frequent credit defaults, or lack of lending experience, their lending limit should be reduced or should be refused for loan services. For financial consumers

[4] (Zhao and Li 2020).

with long-term lending needs, the Internet consumer finance platform may pay attention to the changes in their risk tolerance, income status, liabilities status, and credit status on a real-time basis and make dynamic adjustments to their grading system.

5.2.3 Improve the Knowledge of Financial Consumers on Consumption and Debt

5.2.3.1 Engage Both Financial Regulators and Financial Institutions

Firstly, financial consumers should fully consider their financial conditions for unnecessary consumption to ensure necessary consumption. Secondly, the liabilities should match the income level and risk tolerance of individuals and families. Thirdly, the interest rate and fee rate should be specified when consumers borrow money through the Internet platform, the relevant information should be stated in the electronic contract, and the financial consumers should be entitled to refuse expenses that are not within the scope of the agreement (Ye and Zhang 2015).

5.2.3.2 Raise the Risk Awareness of Financial Consumers to Excessive Debt

Firstly, excessive debt will lead to colossal living pressure and financial pressure on individuals and families, affecting personal health and family harmony. Especially when emergencies occur, it is likely to impact individuals and families seriously. Secondly, once the capital chain is broken and repayment is overdue, there will be a bad record in personal credit information, leading to many adverse effects on their future life, education, employment, etc. Finally, when the group of people with excessive debt expands, it will impact financial stability and even social stability, which may cause the outbreak of a financial crisis (Li 2016).

5.2.4 Regulate Inappropriate Interventions by Internet Platforms

Illegal marketing and publicity of Internet consumer finance platforms will not only mislead financial consumers but also bring reputation risks to the platforms themselves, detrimental to the healthy development of the entire Internet consumer finance sector. Furthermore, as strict supervision gradually becomes the leading tone of financial supervision, Internet consumer finance platforms will face more stringent compliance requirements. Therefore, they must enhance their marketing and publicity compliance capacity.

- Strengthen the monitoring and supervision of the advertising activities of Internet consumer finance platforms, and review the authenticity and legality of the relevant consumer financial products and services provided by these platforms.
- Impose heavier punishments for the illegal marketing of Internet consumer finance platforms. The relevant authorities should issue hefty fines and warnings to the institutions involved and consider imposing punishing measures such as fines and prohibition from practice to responsible persons.
- In order to reduce the misleading and intervention to financial consumers, excessive packaging should be avoided, which dresses the "excessive debt" in the name of "free consumption," luring financial consumers into the "loan trap"; disguising concepts and marking loan products as necessities in marketing should also be avoided, which draws the young and low-income groups into loans through "labeling and slogans."

5.2.5 *Strengthen Data Sharing to Address Data Monopoly and Data Silos*

On the one hand, there needs to be more motivated to share the data among the Internet consumer finance platforms. In particular, the head platforms of some industries control the vast amounts of information and data of financial consumers, which can quickly form a "data monopoly." On the other hand, the understanding, definition, collection, sorting out, and storage of the information and data among different Internet consumer finance platforms are further, which makes the data difficult to be shared and causes the problem of "data silos." One of the key points to solve the problem of excessive debt caused by Internet consumer finance is to find a way to break the dilemma of "borrowing new money to repay old ones, and borrowing for refinancing." Financial authorities could take the lead in formulating financial data standards, regulate the collection, sorting out, storage, and use of economic data, and gradually solve the problems of "data monopoly" and "data silos" by using the shared information on the financial consumers' lending balance information as a breakthrough. Especially for the young and low-income groups who frequently borrow money, risk warnings should be given to the Internet consumer finance platforms when their debt reaches the risk thresholds through the sharing of their lending balance and other information.[5]

5.2.6 *Apply Regulatory Sandbox in Internet Consumer Finance*

Regulatory Sandbox may play an essential role in solving the security and applicability of the applications of Big Data, AI, and other information technologies in Internet consumer finance. The FCA first proposed the "Regulatory Sandbox"

[5] (Zhao 2019).

concept in the United Kingdom. In response to the risks posed by Fintech, the UK has created a "safe space" from the actual market, in which innovative financial products and services can be tested to assess their risks, striking a balance between encouraging the development of Fintech and mitigating the risks of economic collapse. Through sandbox testing, comprehensive and in-depth observations can be made on applying information technology in designing, risk control, marketing, post-loan management, and operation management of Internet consumer finance products. Technical defects can be detected and corrected promptly. As a result, the time spent from innovation to application can be effectively shortened. Judging whether Big Data, AI, and other information technologies can have a positive "chemical reaction" with Internet consumer finance products is possible. The sandbox testing can also test whether the application of information technology will infringe upon the rights and interests of financial consumers and detect technical loopholes that may cause risks and obstruct financial services from achieving universal benefits. In addition, sandbox testing can control the risks and safety issues that may arise from applying information technology in Internet consumer finance within an acceptable range, and it is convenient for regulators to monitor and analyze the operation of "technology plus consumer finance."

5.2.7 Monitor and Manage Internet Consumer Finance Platforms in Real-Time

Although the innovation and application of information technology may bring new risks and problems to the Internet consumer finance sector, it should be clearly understood that "technology is inherently good," and the rights and interests of financial consumers are ultimately infringed upon by the Internet consumer finance platforms which provide financial services through the use of information technology. Given this, it is necessary to use SupTech technologies to carry out real-time monitoring of the operational activities of the Internet consumer finance platforms, establish a cloud platform for the Internet consumer finance sector for real-time monitoring and management, collect operation information on Internet consumer finance platforms with the help of the Big Data platform, use model technology to find out abnormal platforms, carry out all-round analysis and handling of the operation risk information, and timely detect and rectify illegal activities, so as to provide assistance in protecting the rights and interests of financial consumers and ensure the healthy and orderly operation of the sector.[6]

[6] (Sun 2020).

References

Dongrong L (2020) Improving consumers digital financial literacy requires multi-party cooperation. Tsinghua Financ Rev (6)
E C (2018) Internet consumer finance: development trends, challenges and countermeasures, issue 3. Southern Finance
Li Y (2016) Protection of financial consumers' rights and interests from the perspective of internet finance. Econ Manag Res (9)
Li W (2021) Do a good job in data governance to strengthen personal privacy protection. Tsinghua Financ Rev (1)
Sun G (Oct 2020) China regulatory science and technology development report. Social Publishing House
The Research Group of the Financial Consumer Protection Bureau of the People's Bank of China (Feb 2021) Research on the protection of consumer financial information on large internet platforms, http://www.pbc.gov.cn/redianzhuanti/118742/4122386/4122510/4187206/index.html
Yang T (2015) Innovation and development of consumer finance in the internet Era. Zhejiang Econ (13)
Ye X (2015) Analysis of the new trend of consumer finance development under the background of internet finance. Credit (6)
Ye M, Zhang Y (2015) Analysis on the protection of internet financial consumers' rights and interests in China. Financ Theory Pract (9)
Zhao D, Li X (2020) Research on financial supervision under the background of FinTech on the perspective of RegTech, no 4. Zhejiang Finance
Zhao D (2019) Ability and inability of RegTech. Tsinghua Financ Rev (5)

Part II
SupTech in China

In China, the development of SupTech is closely related to the country's regulatory reform and innovation in the financial sector. The Chinese government has been promoting the development of SupTech since 2015 when the China Banking Regulatory Commission established a "FinTech and RegTech Development Plan" to promote the application of new technologies in financial regulation.

Since then, China has made significant progress in SupTech, and a number of SupTech companies have emerged in the country, such as Qulian Technology, FinTalent, and Beijing JD Finance Technology. These companies provide solutions for regulatory compliance, risk management, and data analysis, among others.

Some examples of how SupTech is being used in China include:

- **Anti-Money Laundering (AML) and Counter-Terrorism Financing (CTF) monitoring**: SupTech tools are used to identify suspicious transactions and potential money laundering activities and monitor individuals and organizations involved in terrorism financing.
- **Risk management and assessment**: SupTech tools are used to analyze data from financial institutions and identify potential risks, such as credit and operational risks.
- **Regulatory reporting and compliance**: SupTech tools are used to automate regulatory reporting processes and ensure compliance with regulations and guidelines.

Overall, SupTech is an integral part of China's financial regulatory system, and its development is expected to continue to play a significant role in improving the efficiency and effectiveness of financial regulation in the country.

Chapter 6
Overview of SupTech

Introduction

Comprehensive and in-depth integration of technology and the financial sector is producing profound changes to financial consumption. On the one hand, the 7 * 24 Internet-based and round-the-clock service channels and relatively low product thresholds have enhanced the availability of financial services in an unprecedented manner, significantly reducing the cost of financial services for financial consumers. The Big Data-based risk assessment for financial consumers and financial product classification and grading has made it possible to personalize and customize financial products and services and enhanced the matching of supply and demand of financial services. Financial institutions have improved operating management, reshaped service models, and innovated product designs by virtue of technology, greatly enhancing the efficiency of financial services. Technology enterprises have begun to rely on their advantages in technology, flow, and scenario to provide financial services "across boundaries," giving financial consumers more investment options. With the help of the Internet and mobile apps, financial consumers can quickly and easily access financial product information and experience of other financial consumers, further reducing the information asymmetry of financial transactions. With the development of technology, more financial consumers can enjoy the dividends brought by financial development.

On the other hand, the rapid development and broader application of technology in the financial sector have also brought a series of risk problems. Technology risks still exist. Information technologies such as Big Data and AI still need to be tested by a complete economic cycle, so it is unknown whether they will bring new risks. Problems such as the over-collection of financial consumers' personal information, amplified information leakage risks, and excessive debts should be addressed, leading to severe challenges in protecting financial consumers' rights and interests. Technology enterprises' provision of financial services "across boundaries" not only accelerates the diversification of the participants of financial services but also further blurs the boundary of financial services, making financial risks more hidden and complicated, more widely and faster spread, increasing the overall vulnerability of

D. Zhao et al., *FinTech and SupTech in China*, Contributions to Finance and Accounting,
https://doi.org/10.1007/978-981-99-5173-4_6

the financial system, the probability of the outbreak of systemic financial risks, and the vulnerability of the financial regulatory system. Given the above, research, exploration, and development of SupTech, i.e. "improving supervision through technology and preventing risks through technology," should become an essential path for the financial regulators to cope with the regulatory challenges brought by the model of "technology plus finance".[1]

6.1 RegTech, SupTech and RegTech

CompTech (short for "Compliance Technology") and SupTech are two terms that are often used in the context of regulatory technology (RegTech). While they both refer to applying technology in regulatory compliance, they have different meanings and applications.

Compliance Technology, or CompTech, refers to using technology to automate and streamline regulatory compliance processes. This can include machine learning, artificial intelligence, and natural language processing to automate compliance monitoring, reporting, and risk management. Financial institutions and other regulated entities typically use CompTech to ensure they meet their regulatory obligations more efficiently and cost-effectively.

SupTech, on the other hand, refers to the use of technology by regulators to supervise and monitor regulated entities. SupTech leverages data analytics, machine learning, and artificial intelligence to monitor compliance, identify potential risks, and inform regulatory decision-making. Regulators typically use SupTech to improve their supervisory activities' efficiency and effectiveness and promote compliance and risk management across regulated entities.

In summary, CompTech is focused on improving compliance processes within regulated entities, while SupTech focuses more on improving the supervisory activities of regulators. Both technologies are essential for promoting regulatory compliance and reducing risk in the financial industry.

6.2 Motive Analysis of SupTech Development

6.2.1 The Need to Improve the Capability of and Reduce Costs for Regulators

After the 2008 international financial crisis, financial regulators worldwide began gradually tightening the regulation by adopting more onerous regulatory rules and complicated regulatory procedures to prevent financial risks and ensure financial

---

[1] (Sun and Zhao 2018).

security. "Strict regulation" has gradually become the theme of financial regulation. However, "strict regulation" cannot be implemented without the support and guarantee of funds, technology, and human resources. As the wave of "technology plus finance" sweeps worldwide, the pace of financial innovation is increasingly accelerated. New financial forms, models, products, and technologies emerge one after another, placing financial regulators, constrained by funds, technology, and human resources, under increasing supervision pressure than ever before.

First of all, with the rapid development of the financial sector, the quantity and scale of financial institutions as well as the quantity and variety of financial products have been increasing far faster than the development speed of the financial regulators. Under the constraints of capital, technology, and human resources, it took time for financial regulation to keep up with the pace of financial innovation. Not only did it cause the effectiveness and timeliness of financial regulation challenging to ensure, but it also placed a heavy regulatory burden on financial regulatory agencies, leaving regulatory gaps formed easily. For example, Beijing has approximately 8,000 "7 + 4 + N" institutions, including 7,200 investment companies. At present, the ratio of regulators of the Beijing Local Financial Supervision and Administration Bureau to the number of regulated institutions is 1: 1000. In the face of a large number of regulated objects and a complex system, it is difficult to achieve the timeliness, penetration, and consistency of regulation only by traditional regulation methods such as manual regulation, manual submission of financial statements and manual on-site inspections. Therefore, to enhance the ability of supervision, we must make full use of Big Data, AI, and other technologies and vigorously develop SupTech.[2]

Second, financial products and services are becoming increasingly complex, which requires financial regulators not only to have the expertise to regulate the existing financial products and services but also to have the ability to predict and judge the risks that future financial innovations may bring about. Especially in the general trend of "technology + finance," financial regulators need compound talents familiar with finance and technology, which undoubtedly brings a new challenge to constructing financial regulators' talent teams.

Last but not least, with the increase of regulatory pressure, financial regulators tend to formulate more complicated regulatory rules and procedures, which not only further increases the regulatory burden and cost but also puts forward newer and higher requirements for financial regulators' human resources and technical levels.

Integrating technology and regulation has provided effective technical solutions for financial regulators to ease regulatory pressure, reduce regulatory costs, and improve regulatory standards. Financial regulators may, by using SupTech, monitor abnormal fluctuations in financial markets in real-time, identify and monitor market operations, collect operation data of financial institutions, establish risk warning and justice system, and timely prevent or intervene in illegal operation of financial institutions, so as to achieve the regulatory objectives of preventing and controlling systemic

[2] (Huo 2019).

financial risks, ensuring stable operation of financial institutions, and protecting the rights and interests of financial consumers.[3]

6.2.2 *The Impact of the CompTech Development*

After the 2008 global financial crisis, financial regulations worldwide have gradually tightened, which has directly caused the compliance cost of financial institutions to increase. In order to adapt to the new regulatory requirements, comply with regulatory policies on AML and other aspects and comply with the relevant regulatory systems, and avoid the vast fines resulting from non-compliance, financial institutions in all countries have increased investment in human resources and capital. Therefore, developing and applying "CompTech" can improve the compliance efficiency of financial institutions.

When AI and machine learning have made significant progress at the application level, they can provide optimized solutions to financial institutions in areas such as enhancing the decision-making level, reducing costs, and resolving compliance issues. AI can essentially replace human staff to help banks detect AML or employee misconduct. Regtech has already been applied in data aggregation, risk modeling, scenario analysis, identity verification, real-time monitoring, etc. Professional Regtech companies can help financial institutions check whether they comply with AML and other regulatory policies through automated analysis of massive public and private data and help financial institutions comply with related regulatory systems by using emerging digital technologies such as Cloud Computing and Big Data to avoid huge fines caused by failure to meet regulatory compliance requirements.[4]

Financial institutions can benefit from CompTech in a number of ways. Some of the key benefits include:

- **Increased efficiency**: CompTech can help automate routine compliance tasks, freeing up staff to focus on more complex issues.
- **Improved accuracy**: By using automated tools to monitor and report on compliance issues, financial institutions can reduce the risk of human error and improve the accuracy of their reporting.
- **Reduced risk**: CompTech can help financial institutions identify potential compliance issues before they become significant problems, reducing the risk of fines, penalties, and reputational damage.
- **Enhanced decision-making**: By providing real-time insights into compliance risks and trends, CompTech can help financial institutions make more informed risk management and strategy decisions.

CompTech is becoming increasingly important for financial institutions as regulatory requirements become increasingly complex and non-compliance costs continue

[3] (Zhao 2019).

[4] (Sun 2018).

to rise. By adopting CompTech solutions, financial institutions can better manage compliance risks, reduce costs, and improve operational efficiency.

As CompTech tools become increasingly advanced, regulators may need to develop more complex SupTech tools to keep up with the changing landscape. This could lead to increased costs and complexity for financial institutions and regulators. Overall, the development of CompTech and SupTech will likely continue to be interconnected, influencing the other in various ways. As regulations and compliance requirements continue to evolve, CompTech and SupTech will likely become increasingly important in the financial industry.

6.2.3 The Impact of FinTech Development

The new risks caused by the application and development of technology in the financial sector and the dissimilation of traditional financial risks are the direct reasons why SupTech has attracted wide attention from financial regulators. On the one hand, the new round of technology-driven financial innovation has accelerated unprecedentedly, breaking through the existing regulatory capacity of financial regulators. "Technology + finance" has, to a certain extent, caused the gathering of risks, led to the frequent occurrence of risk events, and increased the fragility of the financial sector. On the other hand, traditional financial institutions and technology companies have invested in Fintech, and technology penetration in the financial sector has reached an unprecedented level. When financial regulators cannot fully understand or know little about new technologies, they often take a negative attitude towards technology innovation in the financial sector because of the need to prevent financial risks, the lack of adequate regulatory measures, and other reasons, resulting in the coexistence of under-regulation and over-regulation. In this context, it is indispensable to use "technology + regulation" to deal with the risks caused by "technology + finance."[5]

Although FinTech and SupTech have different objectives, they are interconnected, and the development of one can affect the development of the other. Here are some ways in which FinTech development could affect SupTech development.

Increased data availability: FinTech companies often collect and analyze large amounts of data to offer personalized and innovative financial products and services. This can provide valuable insights into financial activities regulators can use to improve financial supervision.

Adoption of new technologies: The adoption of new technologies by FinTech companies, such as artificial intelligence and Blockchain, could lead to more sophisticated fraud detection and prevention methods. In addition, regulators could also use these technologies to improve their supervisory functions.

Changes in the financial landscape: FinTech is disrupting traditional financial services, which could lead to changes in the financial landscape. This could require

[5] (Zhao and Li 2020).

regulators to adapt to new technologies and supervise new types of financial activities, such as peer-to-peer lending and crowdfunding.

Collaboration between FinTech and SupTech: FinTech and SupTech companies could collaborate to develop new technologies that benefit both industries. For example, a FinTech company could develop a new technology allowing consumers to share their financial data with multiple institutions securely. In contrast, a SupTech company could develop a tool that monitors the use of this technology to ensure compliance with regulatory requirements.

Overall, the development of FinTech could lead to new challenges and opportunities for SupTech, and collaboration between the two industries could lead to the development of innovative solutions that benefit both. The development and application of SupTech enable financial regulators to have a more comprehensive and in-depth understanding of the operation mechanism, structure, advantages, and disadvantages of technologies, as well as the combination with financial business, which makes it easier to locate the risks brought by technologies to financial innovation. Therefore, financial regulators can then use technologies to arm regulation, supplement regulatory weakness, and diversify regulatory approaches.

6.2.4 Activation from Modern Information Technologies

China is in a critical period of financial risk prevention and control, which is the fundamental task of China's financial regulatory efforts. At the Fifth National Financial Work Conference, President Xi pointed out that "prevention of systemic financial risks is the eternal theme of financial work, and we should put active prevention and resolution of systemic financial risks in a more critical position, conduct scientific prevention, and early identification, early warning, early detection, and early disposal, focus on prevention and resolution of risks in critical fields, and focus on improving financial security defense line and risk emergency response mechanism." It not only points out the direction and the focus of the future development of financial regulation but also puts forward higher and newer requirements for financial SupTech and means.

With the breakthroughs in the development of modern information technologies such as Internet, Big Data, Cloud Computing, AI, and Blockchain, the capabilities of financial regulators to prevent, control, judge, assess, and dispose of financial risks have been enhanced. Firstly, the Internet is an essential channel for financial regulators to obtain data and information and the underlying "platform" for achieving data and information sharing and information disclosure. It is also the cornerstone for applying Big Data, AI, and Blockchain. Secondly, financial regulators can use Big Data technology to achieve automatic data collection, extraction, cleaning, conversion, processing, application, and sharing and provide data-based means for decision-making.

Furthermore, with the help of the cloud platform, financial regulators can integrate the financial regulatory business of multiple lines and multiple systems and make judgments and forecasts of economic and financial operations from a more comprehensive and systematic perspective. Thirdly, financial regulators can also use technologies such as AI and risk models to paint a precise "portrait" of financial institutions, comprehensively and accurately reflect the risk profile of financial institutions, timely give risk warnings, further improve regulatory efficiency utilizing ex-ante risk management, and also provide a basis for financial supervision and on-site law enforcement inspections. Fourthly, financial regulators can also, by virtue of Blockchain technology, allow part of financial business to be "on-chain" and achieve breakthroughs in smart contracts (automatic execution), transaction tracking, information protection, etc.

6.3 Concept and Connotation of SupTech

From SupTech's conception germination to its application, financial regulators and international financial organizations worldwide have defined SupTech from different perspectives. However, the sector and academia have yet to reach a unified consensus on the concept of SupTech.

6.3.1 Definition of SupTech by Financial Regulators and International Organizations

The FCA of the UK defines SupTech as promoting compliance by financial institutions and believes that SupTech is a branch of FinTech that focuses on a range of technologies that can meet regulatory requirements more efficiently and effectively.[6]

The Financial sector Regulatory Authority (FINRA) of the US points out in the publication of Technology-Based Innovations for Regulatory Compliance in the Securities sector that "RegTech is a term that has not been universally defined, and generally refers to innovative technologies designed to enable financial institutions to fulfill their regulatory compliance obligations." Michael S. Piwowar, then acting chairman of the Securities and Exchange Commission, put forward in his speech at the 2018 RegTech Data Summit that "RegTech is the use of technology by financial regulators to fulfill their regulatory responsibilities more comprehensively and efficiently."[7,8]

The Australian Securities and Investments Commission (ASIC) states that "RegTech has great potential to help companies build a culture of compliance,

[6] Financial Conduct Authority (Jul 2016) Call for input on supporting the development and adoption of RegTech, Feedback statement.

[7] The Financial Industry Regulatory Authority (Sep 2018) Technology based innovation for regulatory compliance ("Regtech") in the security industry.

[8] (Piwowar 2018).

identify learning opportunities, and save on the costs (both time and money) of compliance."

The Monetary Authority of Singapore (MAS) states, "RegTech is the use of technical means to strengthen the risk management and compliance of financial institutions" (Monetary Authority of Singapore 2019).

The Institute of International Finance (IIF) defines RegTech as "new technologies that can efficiently and effectively satisfy regulatory and compliance requirements."[9]

The Bank for International Settlements (BIS) uses the term "Supervisory Technology (SupTech)" in its book Technical Innovation in Financial Supervision: Experiences from Early Practitioners and defines it as "the use of technical innovation by regulators in support of regulation and the methodology enabling regulators to digitize supervisory reporting and the supervisory process for more effective and proactive monitoring of risks and compliance status of financial institutions."[10]

The World Bank (WB), in its Roadmap of SupTech for Low-income Countries, points out that "SupTech is the use of technology to improve and strengthen the financial supervision process from the perspective of the regulator, and RegTech is the compliance process managed by the financial sector through technical means."[11]

In summary, financial regulators and international financial organizations worldwide have not reached a unified understanding of the concept of SupTech. The financial regulators of the UK, the US, Australia, Singapore, and other countries understand RegTech more from the compliance perspective, emphasizing the vital role played by technology in assisting financial institutions in complying effectively with regulatory requirements. By contrast, international financial organizations define RegTech more from the perspective of financial supervision, considering technology as a practical path to regulatory innovation.

6.3.2 Definition of SupTech by Financial Regulators in China

In May 2017, the Fintech Committee of the PBOC proposed that "SupTech should be strengthened, and the Big Data, AI, Cloud Computing should be actively used to enrich financial supervision tools, so as to enhance the capabilities of screening, preventing and resolving cross-sector and cross-market financial risks."

According to Sun Guofeng, then director of the Institute of Finance of the PBOC (2017), RegTech is "an organic combination of technology and supervision, mainly playing a role in using technology to help financial institutions meet regulatory compliance requirements." In his follow-up research (2018), it was pointed out that the SupTech refers to the emerging technologies represented by Big Data, Cloud

[9] Institute of International Finance (Mar 2016) RegTech in financial services: solutions for compliance and reporting.

[10] Bank for International Settlements (Jul 2018) Innovative Technology in Financial Supervision (SupTech)-The Experience of Early Users.

[11] World Bank Group (Dec 2020) A roadmap of SupTech solutions to low income (IDA) countries.

Computing, AI, Blockchain, etc., mainly utilized to maintain the safety and stability of the financial system to realize the proper operation of financial institutions and to protect the rights of financial consumers. From the application perspective, Regtech and SupTech show compliance and regulation functions, respectively. Regtech is, for Financial institutions, an essential means and tool to reduce compliance costs and adapt to regulation, and it can be interpreted as CompTech in this regard. On the other hand, SupTech is for financial regulators to enrich their regulatory methods, improve their regulatory efficiency and reduce the regulatory pressure they face, which is a meaningful way to safeguard the safety and stability of the financial system, prevent systemic financial risks and protect the rights and interests of financial consumers.[12,13].

Li Wei, general director of the Department of Science and Technology of the PBOC, believes that the nature of SupTech, as an essential branch of FinTech, is to adopt new technologies to establish reliable, sustainable, and enforceable regulatory agreements and compliance assessment mechanisms between regulators and financial institutions, aiming to improve the regulatory efficiency of regulators and reduce the compliance costs of financial institutions. From the perspective of regulation, financial regulators, through the application of Big Data, Cloud Computing, and AI, can better perceive trends of financial risks, enhance the real-time collection, integration, and sharing of regulatory data, effectively detect illegal operations, high-risk transactions, and other potential problems, and improve the accuracy of risk identification and the effectiveness of risk prevention. From the compliance perspective, financial institutions adopt methods such as application connection and system embedding to "translate" rules, regulations, regulatory policies, and compliance requirements into digital protocols to reduce manual intervention utilizing automation and ambiguity in understanding employing standardization, make operation and implementation more efficient, convenient and accurate, effectively reduce compliance costs and enhance compliance efficiency.[14]

In August 2018, the CSRC ("CSRC") issued the Overall Construction Plan for SupTech (the "Plan"), indicating the completion of the high-level design of the SupTech construction of CSRC and the beginning of the comprehensive implementation stage. The Plan states, "SupTech is to provide CSRC with comprehensive and accurate data and analysis services through Big Data, Cloud Computing, and AI, based on electronic and network supervision."[15]

In August 2020, Zhou Liang, vice chairman of the CBIRC, pointed out in his article Improving Corporate Governance and Promoting High-quality Development of Joint-Stock Banks, the need to vigorously develop SupTech, explore the application

---

[12] (Sun 2017).

[13] (Sun 2018).

[14] (Li 2017).

[15] CSRC (Aug, 2018): CSRC Formally Publishes and Implements the Overall Construction Plan of SupTech, http://www.csrc.gov.cn/pub/newsite/zjhxwfb/xwdd/201808/t20180831_343433.html

of Big Data, Cloud Computing, and AI to improve the way and means of corporate governance regulation, and enhance the level of digitalization of regulation".[16]

In November 2019, Li Dongrong, president of the National Internet Finance Association of China, said at the Beijing International Financial Security Forum 2019, "SupTech is increasingly becoming a global focus of attention of many parties such as financial regulators, financial institutions, and technology companies. From the regulation perspective, SupTech uses various technological means to effectively optimize the regulatory process and continuously improve regulatory efficiency with financial regulatory data as basic elements, to achieve the goal of financial regulation with higher efficiency and lower cost."[17]

In July 2019, Huo Xuewen, general director of Beijing Local Financial Supervision and Management Bureau, pointed out that "historically, the development of the financial sector is inseparable from technological innovation. On the one hand, every science and technology revolution results from the inventions of new financial regimes and mechanisms, new markets, and new products. On the other hand, science and technology are also constantly driving the changes in the financial sector. The global financial business has gone through stages of e-information finance, internet finance, Fintech, intelligent Finance, etc. SupTech will become an advanced form of Fintech innovation and institutional reform.[18]

6.3.3 *Definition of SupTech by Scholars in China*

The current academic circles have yet to form a clear consensus over the concept of Regtech. Yang (2015), from the Law School of Renmin University of China, believed that RegTech is the methodology of "technology-driven regulation," which refers to the introduction of a technology dimension in addition to such traditional regulatory dimensions as prudential regulation and conduct regulation, to form a two-dimensional regulatory system.[19]

Hu (2017), from the Institute of Finance of the Chinese Academy of Social Sciences, pointed out that SupTech is devoted to applying emerging technology in the financial system, especially in micro areas, to meet regulatory standards and compliance requirements better. SupTech is supposed to realize regulatory compliance by a technical force. However, it also shows a tendency that SupTech can also be leveraged to avoid the regulation.[20]

Yin (2019), from the Institute of Finance of the Chinese Academy of Social Sciences, pointed out that RegTech consists of SupTech and Comptech and is to reform financial regulation through science and technology, to assist regulators

[16] (Zhao 2020).
[17] (Li 2019).
[18] (Huo 2019).
[19] (Yang 2015).
[20] (Hu 2017).

through optimizing regulatory methods, to help financial institutions reduce compliance costs, and to balance regulation and innovation, so as to achieve the goal of stable and healthy development of the financial sector. In a narrow sense, SupTech is a branch of FinTech, focusing on monitoring, identifying, preventing, and controlling financial risks brought by FinTech, constructing the FinTech ecosystem, and promoting the steady and healthy development of FinTech. In a broader sense, SupTech is a variety of IT applications and solutions that help companies deal with regulatory compliance and risk control issues throughout the financial system. The potential value of Regtech is more than reducing the compliance costs for financial institutions, as they facilitate the establishment of a set of regulatory regimes for the real-time monitoring of financial operations and the identification, assessment, and management of risks.[21]

Ba (2020), from the HSBC Institute for Financial Studies of Peking University, regarded RegTech as a branch of Fintech, enjoying remarkable development momentum in recent years. In his opinion, RegTech consists of two aspects: (1) CompTech services provided by CompTech enterprises based on AI and Big Data analysis, etc., for financial institutions for compliance management; (2) SupTech leveraged by regulators to strengthen their regulation and supervision capacity.[22]

He 2018, president of Jingdong Financial Research Institute, regarded RegTech as a value-oriented solution based on more efficient compliance and more effective regulation in the context of a closer combination of finance and technology, driven by data as the core, based on Cloud Computing, AI, Blockchain, etc. In his opinion, there are two branches of RegTech, SupTech for regulators' supervision and CompTech for financial institutions' compliance. In other words, RegTech = SupTech + CompTech.[23]

6.3.4 Connotation of SupTech

Based on the definitions of SupTech discussed above, as well as the analysis from the perspective of the progress and application of SupTech in China, this book hereto concludes that SupTech can be summarized as a technical tool, means, or system which to improve the supervision level of financial regulators and to help financial institutions better meet the regulatory requirements, through modern information technologies such as Big Data, Cloud Computing, AI, Blockchain.[24]

Since the 2008 global financial crisis, the developed countries led by the US have gradually changed their thoughts on financial regulation. Through legislation,

[21] (Yin 2019).

[22] (Ba 2020).

[23] (He 2018).

[24] Except as otherwise noted, the term "SupTech" mentioned in the subsequent research of this book only refers to "SupTech.".

remodeling the financial regulatory framework, and reforming the financial regulatory system, these countries have fully practiced strict regulation and prevented systemic financial risks to improve their entire financial regulatory system. In the UK, US, Australia, Singapore, etc., the concept of RegTech was first derived from financial institutions' compliance needs, where the financial regulators' role mainly encourages financial institutions to carry out technology innovation and improve compliance capability by clarifying regulatory requirements.

From the financial regulation and supervision practice history, China's previous financial regulators were more tolerant of financial institutions. As a result, they tended to provide a relatively loose regulatory environment for the innovation and development of financial institutions. However, with the rapid development of the financial sector, especially with the emergence of new financial forms such as internet finance and FinTech, the pace of financial innovation has exceeded the scope of financial regulation, which has posed a considerable challenge to China's financial regulators. Meanwhile, preventing and controlling financial risks and safeguarding national financial security have become and will continue to become vital for China's regulators in recent years and in the future. Therefore, the development of SupTech in China will focus more on comprehensively leveraging Big Data, Cloud Computing, AI, Blockchain, and other technologies to improve regulation and supervision, optimize the regulatory process, enhance regulatory efficiency, and achieve regulatory goals.

As discussed above, SupTech and CompTech are two subsets of RegTech. Financial regulators and institutions use technology on a large scale to arm regulation and compliance work concurrently. As a result, financial regulation goals such as preventing financial risks, safeguarding the sound operation of financial institutions, and protecting financial consumers will be better met. (as shown in Fig. 6.1).

This book believes that the development path should be determined before constructing a RegTech system nationwide. RegTech mainly involves financial regulators, institutions, SupTech Companies, and Fintech Companies. SupTech Companies and Fintech Companies, as the development bodies of RegTech, provide RegTech support based on emerging information technologies such as Big Data, Cloud Computing, AI, distributed ledger, biometrics, and digital encryption. As the application bodies of RegTech, financial regulators and financial institutions would use RegTech to enrich regulatory methods, enhance the level of financial regulation, meet regulatory requirements, and reduce compliance costs. It is imperative to rationalize the relationship among the various subjects involved in the RegTech ecosystem, to effectively coordinate the regulatory demand, compliance demand, and technology supply, and to form a virtuous cycle conducive to the development of RegTech. The R&D of RegTech contains three paths: independent development, technology outsourcing, and technology cooperation (as shown in Fig. 6.2).

The first path is developing independently. Financial regulators are likely to be constrained by three aspects: technology, capital, and personnel. There are many obstacles in the independent development of SupTech, especially for local financial regulators. In terms of technology, financial regulators focus on financial regulation, with a lack of in-depth research on the core algorithms and operating mechanisms of

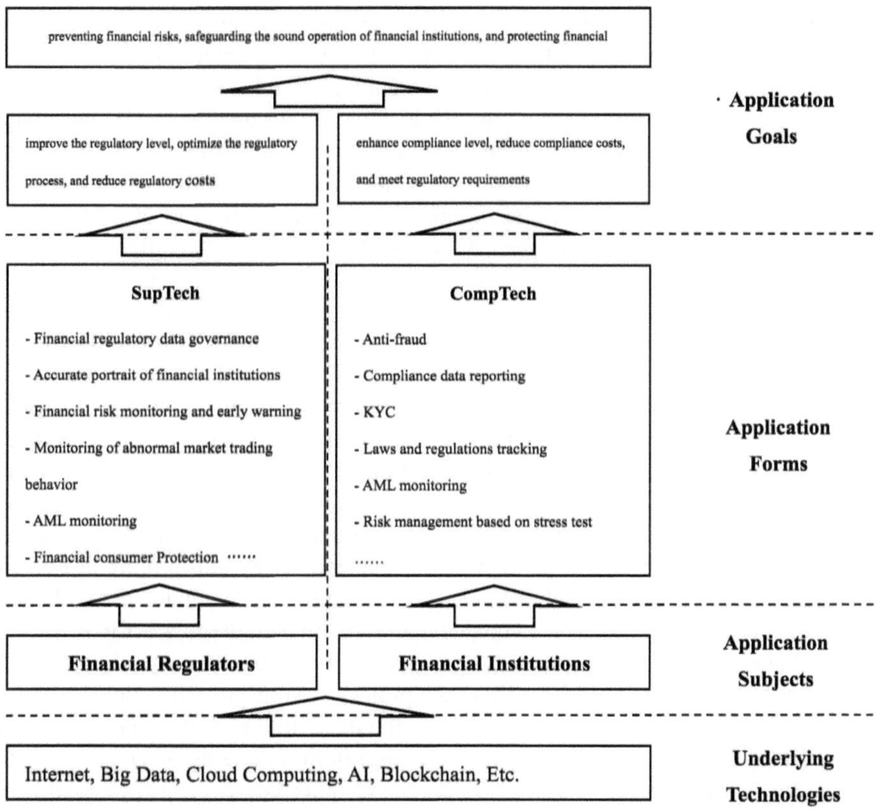

Fig. 6.1 SupTech & CompTech

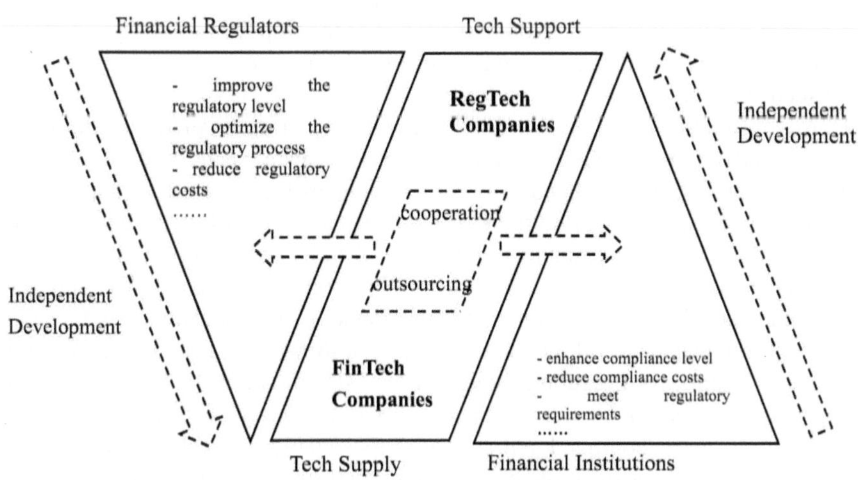

Fig. 6.2 Respective development model of SupTech and CompTech

Big Data, Cloud Computing, AI, Blockchain, etc. For example, financial regulators independently developing SupTech may need help with problems such as lagging in technical updates, mismatching between technical systems and regulatory needs, and repetitive investment due to a long R&D cycle. In terms of capital, inadequate capital guarantees and low utilization rates may directly lead to the inability of the SupTech system to meet the needs of financial regulation effectively. In terms of personnel, financial regulators have weak links in the cultivation of science and technology talents, the gap between financial regulators and their R&D teams in terms of number, quality, and talent structure remains significant, and the SupTech R&D teams face the risk of brain drain. In particular, the flow of the compound talents in finance and technology after long-term cultivation into financial institutions will affect the effectiveness of financial regulation in a short period.

The second path is technology outsourcing. For financial regulators, this path may trigger new risk problems. When Fintech companies (or the RegTech companies whose related parties are financial institutions) export the SupTech system to the financial regulators, they will likely become "implicit regulators". Therefore, in terms of SupTech development, adopting technology cooperation can avoid various obstacles and risks arising from independent R&D and technology outsourcing. Based on the regulatory requirements and technology needs raised by the financial regulators, the Fintech companies (or RTT companies) and the financial regulators may jointly carry out the R&D of the SupTech system. The technical personnel of the financial regulators should participate throughout the project, design, structure, development, and other links of the SupTech system. After the R&D of the system, a professional third-party institution should verify the core algorithm, operating mechanism, code design, business module, operation process, and other contents of the system. In addition, in order to avoid setting up technical "back doors" and use of loopholes in the SupTech system to escape regulation, financial regulators should impose strict restrictions on Fintech companies and their related parties (or RTT companies and their related parties) that participate in the R&D of the SupTech system to carry out their business activities in the relevant financial industries subject to the supervision of the such system.

Thirdly, pressure from competition and regulation gives financial institutions a natural incentive to use technology to improve compliance business. With the deepening of the R&D and application of CompTech, in the absence of supervision and guidance, financial institutions will inevitably use technology to avoid supervision and even look for regulatory loopholes, thereby reducing the effectiveness of financial supervision, leading to vicious competition among financial institutions, damaging the development environment of the financial sector and affecting financial stability. Given this, the development of CompTech should be based on precise regulatory requirements, formulation of standards and specifications for CompTech, and appropriate participation by financial regulators in the R&D of CompTech. Financial institutions are encouraged and guided to reasonably use technological means to give full play to the critical role of technology in promoting quality improvement, efficiency improvement, and inclusive development of the financial sector.

China is undergoing a crucial period of prevention and control of financial risks. The CPC and the Chinese government have repeatedly stressed the importance of preventing and controlling financial risks, protecting national financial security, and maintaining financial stability. The 19th National Congress of the CPC, the 2017 Central Economic Work Conference, and the Fifth National Financial Work Conference have raised higher requirements for the financial sector's stability, development, and reform. On the one hand, financial regulators are under pressure brought by backwardness in SupTech development and regulation gaps caused by heavy regulatory tasks and unreasonable regulatory systems; on the other hand, in order to adapt to strict regulatory requirements, financial institutions also need to pay more costs for compliance.

In this context, in order to win the battle of prevention and control of financial risks, effectively play the vital role of SupTech in preventing financial risks and assisting in the construction of a new financial ecology, it is necessary to give priority to the development of SupTech system for a few areas with relatively major risks, such as liquidity risk identification and prevention, shadow banking regulation, intelligent investment advisory regulation, illegal fund-raising monitoring, and KYD, to comprehensively monitoring and preventing the financial risks.

6.4 Retrospect and Prospect of China's SupTech Market

Comptech and SupTech are becoming increasingly important in China's financial industry as they enable financial institutions to comply with regulatory requirements more efficiently and effectively, improving their overall risk management capabilities.

According to a report by the Asian Development Bank in 2021, the Comptech market in China was expected to reach $27.4 billion by 2025, growing at a CAGR of 29.1% from 2020 to 2025. In addition, the report also states that China's SupTech market is proliferating, driven by the need for effective regulatory oversight in the financial sector. The SupTech market in China was estimated to be worth around $2.2 billion in 2020 and was expected to grow at a CAGR of 25.9% from 2020 to 2025.

In the early stages, China's SupTech market was mainly focused on regulatory compliance and risk management. As a result, the market was dominated by traditional financial institutions, and there needed to be more competition from new players. However, China's SupTech market has experienced rapid growth in the past few years. Technological advancements, increased regulatory scrutiny, and the entry of new players into the market have driven this growth. As a result, the market has expanded beyond traditional financial institutions, including fintech companies, data analytics firms, and AI startups. Regarding regulatory collaboration, regulators in China have been actively collaborating with SupTech companies to promote innovation in the financial industry. This collaboration has led to the development of new technologies and the adoption of new regulatory frameworks.

In conclusion, China's SupTech market has experienced significant growth in recent years, and the future looks bright. With the increasing adoption of new technologies and the expanding regulatory framework, the SupTech market is poised to play a critical role in shaping the future of the financial industry in China and beyond.

References

Ba S, Hu L, Zhu Y (2020) Australian regulatory technology: current situation and experience, no 4. Economic and Social Comparison

He H, Yin D, Liu Y (2018) SupTech: research on connotation, application and development trend, no 10. Research on Financial Supervision

Hu B (2017) Regulatory technology is approaching, no 11. Contemporary Financier

Huo X (2019) Vigorously develop regulatory technology to help local financial supervision, no 5. Tsinghua Financial Review

Institute of International Finance (Mar 2016) RegTech in financial services: solutions for compliance and reporting

Li W (2017) Fintech development and supervision, no 8. China Finance

Li D (Nov 18, 2019) Developing SupTech is a Strong Support to Maintain Financial Security under the New Situation. Securities Daily

Monetary Authority of Singapore (Mar 2019) Consultation paper on proposed revisions to business continuity management guidelines

Piwowar MS (Mar 2018) Remarks at the 2018 RegTech data summit-old fields. New Corn: Innovation in Technology and Law

Sun G (2017) From FinTech to RegTech. Tsinghua Financ Rev (5)

Sun G (2018) Developing regulatory technology to build a new financial ecology. Tsinghua Financ Rev (3)

Sun G, Zhao D (2018) Challenges and Breakthroughs of SupTech. China Finance (21)

Yang D (2015) Regulatory technology: regulatory challenges and dimension reconstruction of fintech. Chin Soc Sci (5)

Yin Z, Fan Y (2019) Theoretical basis, practical application and development suggestions of RegTech. Financial Law (3)

Zhao D (2019) Ability and inability of RegTech. Tsinghua Financ Rev (5)

Zhou L (2020) Improving Corporate Governance and Promoting High-quality Development of Joint-Stock Banks. Research on Financial Regulation (7)

Zhao D, Li X (2020) Research on financial supervision under the background of FinTech on the perspective of RegTech, no 4. Zhejiang Finance

Chapter 7
Theoretical Issues and Concerns Around SupTech

Introduction

As discussed in Chap. 6, the practitioners, and academia have not yet established a comprehensive theoretical system for SupTech, leaving many fundamental theoretical issues unsolved. In particular, the connotation and scope of SupTech still in controversies and need further clarifies. Therefore, it is of great value and practical significance to clarify the fundamental theoretical issues of SupTech.

7.1 Fundamental Theoretical Issues Around SupTech

- **Privacy and Data Protection**: SupTech lives on data, including sensitive financial and personal information. As such, data breaches, unauthorized access, and data misuse are likely to occur. Therefore, regulators must ensure that appropriate data protection measures are in place to protect the privacy and confidentiality of data and personal information.
- **Bias and Fairness**: The algorithms and machine learning models used in SupTech, concerning their performance, are closely related to the trained data. Bias in the data and algorithms could lead to unfair outcomes or discrimination. Regulators must ensure that SupTech tools are helpful under testing to minimize bias and ensure fairness.
- **Accountability and Transparency**: SupTech can automate many supervisory tasks to reduce the need for human intervention. However, SupTech also raises questions about accountability and transparency. Regulators need to ensure that there is clear accountability for the decisions made by SupTech tools and that there is transparency around the data and algorithms used.
- **Regulatory Arbitrage**: SupTech can enable financial institutions to identify and exploit regulatory loopholes. Regulators must be aware of the potential for regulatory arbitrage and ensure that SupTech tools effectively prevent it.

D. Zhao et al., *FinTech and SupTech in China*, Contributions to Finance and Accounting,
https://doi.org/10.1007/978-981-99-5173-4_7

- **Adoption and Integration**: The success of SupTech relies on its adoption and integration into existing regulatory frameworks. However, there may be resistance to change and technical and organizational challenges to overcome. Therefore, regulators must ensure that SupTech tools are user-friendly, accessible, and integrated seamlessly into existing regulatory processes.

Addressing these theoretical issues is crucial for successfully implementing and adopting SupTech in financial regulation.

7.2 Underlying Technologies of SupTech

Big Data, Cloud Computing, AI, and Blockchain can be technological means used to improve financial regulation. In nature, technology is a tool to improve the service efficiency of the industry, innovate products, and optimize the operating processes of institutions. On the one hand, when these modern information technologies do not serve financial regulation, they should not be labeled as part of financial regulation. On the other hand, these modern information technologies can be applied in the financial sector and developed in integration with other industries. For example, when combined with the financial business, these technologies give birth to Fintech; when applied in the cultural industry, they may give birth to cultural technology; and when integrated with the educational industry, they may give birth to educational technology.

The underlying technologies of SupTech include:

- **Big Data Analytics**: The use of Big Data analytics helps regulatory authorities analyze large volumes of data from various sources in real time, enabling them to detect potential risks and identify compliance issues more quickly.
- **AI**: AI automates regulatory compliance monitoring and risk management processes. AI algorithms can detect patterns and anomalies in large datasets to enable regulators to identify potential risks and improve supervisory efficiency (Zhao and Li 2021).
- **Blockchain**: Blockchain technology offers secure and transparent data-sharing capabilities, which can be helpful for regulators and supervised entities to share information efficiently, securely, and with minimum trust requirements.
- **Cloud Computing**: Cloud Computing enables regulators to store, process, and analyze large amounts of data from different sources in a cost-effective and scalable way. Cloud-based solutions also offer more secure and reliable storage solutions.
- **Machine Learning**: Machine learning is a subfield of AI that focuses on enabling machines to learn from data without explicit programming. ML algorithms can detect patterns and anomalies in large datasets, enabling regulators to identify potential risks and improve supervisory efficiency.

- **Natural Language Processing (NLP)**: NLP is a subfield of AI that focuses on the interaction between computers and humans in natural language. NLP can be used to analyze textual data, such as regulatory filings, and identify potential compliance issues.
- **Robotics and Automation**: Robotics and automation technologies can automate regulatory processes such as data entry, data verification, and report generation, thereby reducing errors and improving efficiency.

SupTech solutions can help regulators and supervised entities make better decisions and improve compliance by leveraging the latest technological innovations.

As stated above, this book defines SupTech as "technological tools, methodologies and systems that are designed to improve the regulatory level of financial regulators through the use of modern information technologies such as Big Data, Cloud Computing, AI and Blockchain." It should be emphasized that the technological tools, methodologies, and systems mentioned in this book are innovative regulatory tools forged as a result of "technology plus financial regulation" in China (see Table 7.1).

As shown in Table 7.1, various platforms and systems developed by financial regulators based on technical means, such as the Internet, Big Data, Cloud Computing, AI, and Blockchain, are the real SupTech for financial regulation. Therefore, it would need to be more accurate to lump modern information technology together with SupTech.

Table 7.1 SupTech programs and underlying technologies

SupTech program	Underlying technologies
PBOC Guiyang central sub-branch: a big-data-supported decision-making platform of the Central Bank	Big data
PBOC Chengdu branch: big data monitoring and analysis system for monetary credit	Big data
PBOC Wuhan branch: information sharing system between financial institutions	APP, PC Software, big data
CBIRC: national platform for risk control and prevention of illegal financial activities	Internet, big data, AI, etc.
CSRC: SupTech system	Internet, big data, cloud computing, and AI
PCAC: sector risk information sharing system, information management system for authorized clients, and management platform for certification and management of FinTech Products	Internet and big data, etc.
NIFA: platforms for Internet finance reporting, information sharing, registration and disclosure, and monitoring of AML and CTF	Internet and big data, etc.

7.2.1 Whether SupTech is a Subset of FinTech?

Both FinTech and SupTech originated in the United Kingdom. As a competent financial regulator in the UK, the Financial Conduct Authority (FCA) provides guidance, promotion, and encouragement for the development of SupTech. FCA's role is to inform financial institutions of the regulatory requirements, foster an overall environment for the development of Fintech and SupTech, formulate SupTech standards and guidelines, and remove barriers to the entry, innovation, and application of SupTech. In addition, financial institutions are responsible for R&D and the application of SupTech. Therefore, SupTech and Fintech are under financial institutions' efforts to introduce modern technologies into the financial service process.

However, as seen from the previous analysis of SupTech, when financial regulators use technology to improve the level of regulation, optimize the regulatory process, and reduce the cost of regulation, it is called SupTech. When financial institutions use technology to enhance compliance, reduce compliance costs, and meet regulatory requirements, it is called CompTech. From this point of view, it is incorrect to regard SupTech as a subset of Fintech (Sun 2017).

7.2.2 SupTech Under the "Technology for Good" Theory

Let us start with analyzing what technology is. Technology is a primary productive force. Throughout the ages, every progress of human society has been accompanied by the progress of science and technology. In particular, the rapid progress of modern technology has opened up a broader space for the development of socially productive forces and human civilization and vigorously promoted the development of the economy and society. The rapid growth of high-tech enterprises in China's computer, telecommunications, biomedicine, new materials, etc., has greatly improved the industrial technology level of China, promoted the substantial increase of industrial and agricultural productivity, and driven the development of the entire national economy. The practice has proved that high-tech industries have become the leading industries of modern economic development. It can be seen that "for good" is the natural and inherent attribute of science and technology.[1]

Second, technology is a double-edged sword. The deep integration of technology and finance has promoted the development of financial inclusion but also brought new risks to the financial sector, led to the dissimilation of traditional financial risks, and formed a severe challenge to financial regulation and supervision. Although technological innovation, transformation, and application have brought new risks to the financial sector, technology is neutral. Most risks in the Fintech sector come from various entities that use technologies to provide financial services. Especially

[1] Science and technology, Baidu Encyclopedia, https://baike.baidu.com/item/%E7%A7%91%E5%AD%A6%E6%8A%80%E6%9C%AF/3348043?Fromtitle=%E7%A7%91%E6%8A%80&fromid=662906&fr=aladdin.

in the slowdown of economic growth, inadequate regulatory measures, and lack of risk awareness of financial consumers, financial institutions operating in regulatory gray areas and illegal business operations are the primary source of the frequent occurrence of risk cases in respect of Fintech. Therefore, financial supervision should focus on rectifying and cracking down on the illegal business operations of financial institutions.

Given this, the guiding principle financial institutions should follow in business is that "technology is inherently good and therefore should be used appropriately." Accordingly, financial regulators should focus on guiding financial institutions to use technology in a "good" way, using technology to facilitate "inclusive and favorable" financial services, rather than to use technology to violate regulations, evade regulation, or obtain illegitimate interests.

7.2.3 *Financial Regulatory Regime Reform and SupTech Regime Establishment*

Currently and shortly, China's financial sector is and will still be in a period where risks occur quickly and frequently. Under multiple onshore and offshore factors, risk points are numerous and broad, presenting the characteristics of obscurity, complexity, suddenness, infectiousness, and harmfulness. The problem of structural imbalance is prominent. Law and regulation violations occur frequently, potential risks and hidden dangers accumulate, and vulnerability increases significantly. The occurrence of "black swan" and "grey rhino" should be prevented. The accumulation of potential financial risks and the financial supervision system based on the concept of "entity regulation are closely connected. In the supervision model of "railway police, each with its management section," regulatory standards are inconsistent for the same type of financial products in different markets, and the same type of financial products distributed online and offline, which not only leaves scope for the supervision arbitrage by financial institutions but also leaves gaps for a large number of non-financial enterprises to engage in financial business illegally.

Therefore, the reform of the financial supervision system should be promoted. At the Fifth National Conference on Financial Work, it is required to adhere to the starting point of national conditions to promote the reform of the financial supervision system, enhance the authoritativeness and effectiveness of financial regulation coordination, and enhance the specialization, unity, and penetration of financial regulation. The 19th National Congress of the CPC put forward the principle of "improving the financial regulatory system and holding the bottom line of non-occurrence of systematic financial risks." The 2017 Central Economic Work Conference stresses that "effectively prevent and dispose of risks in key fields, resolutely crack down on illegal and irregular financial activities, and strengthen the construction of regulatory systems for weak links."

Promoting the reform of the financial regulatory system is to prevent financial risks. However, the boundary between financial products and business is blurred based on financial innovation, and cross-market, cross-business type, cross-region shadow banking, and illegal criminal risks increase, all directly related to the lack of regulatory capacity. Therefore, to prevent and control significant risks, it is necessary to promote the reform of the financial regulatory system and change the current regulation concept and promote the innovation of financial supervision technology. It is the key to developing SupTech to improve financial supervision, respond to financial innovation, and prevent financial risks. While promoting the development of SupTech to prevent and control financial risks, we also see the limitations of SupTech, i.e., SupTech can only partially solve the problem of the restraint mechanism of regulators with the promotion of financial regulatory system reform.[2]

7.3 Unsolved Problems and Development Difficulties Facing SupTech

7.3.1 Coexistence of Data Monopoly and Data Silos

On the one hand, due to the needs of business competition and cost control, financial institutions lack motivation to share data, especially for some Fintech companies, who hold a large amount of personal information and behavioral data of customers through social software, shopping software, and payment tools, which will quickly form data monopoly. On the other hand, financial regulators and financial institutions understand, define, collect, sort out, and store data independently, making it difficult to share such data. Furthermore, even concerning the same data, financial regulators and financial institutions may process data differently due to their different positions and perspectives. Therefore, it makes data an isolated island physically and logically and increases the communication cost for financial regulators and institutions to cooperate in data sharing and cooperation. With precise requirements from the financial regulators for data reporting or the motivation for data sharing, SupTech will be able to break the current data monopoly and data island problems, which will also cause some SupTech applications based on Big Data technologies to lack credibility and comparability (Sun 2019).

[2] (Sun 2019).

7.3.2 FinTech Companies Play as Athletes and Referees Simultaneously

From the perspective of the development path of SupTech, both Fintech companies and professional SupTech companies can be the providers of SupTech tools, techniques, and systems. However, suppose SupTech research and SupTech development are both undertaken by Fintech companies, the phenomenon of "being both athletes and referees" could occur and Fintech companies are likely to become "hidden regulators."

Given that there are many obstacles in the in-house development of SupTech by the financial regulators in terms of systems, mechanisms, personnel, funds, and technical supports, it is a relatively appropriate development path for the financial regulators to put forward the regulatory requirements and the market to provide the SupTech services. However, it is noteworthy that in the R&D and application of SupTech, it is complicated for financial regulators to master core algorithms and rules of Big Data, Cloud Computing, AI, machine learning, etc. If Fintech companies provide SupTech services, it will be inevitable that FinTech Companies will have more financial data and regulatory data at their disposal. In addition, FinTech Companies have already collected customers' personal information and behavioral data. It will not only further aggravate data monopoly, but also provide Fintech Companies with the opportunities to find loopholes in SupTech and even create "back doors" for themselves, which may lead to Fintech Companies' avoidance of regulation and even affect regulation (Sun 2020).

7.3.3 SupTech Cannot Replace Regulators in Making Decisions

Although SupTech has excellent potential in relieving the current regulatory pressure, enhancing efficiency, improving the level of regulation, and providing valuable support to regulatory decision-making, it cannot replace the role of regulators in making informed and contextualized decisions that balance the interests of different stakeholders and comply with legal and ethical standards.

- **Human judgment**: Regulators use their expertise and experience to make informed decisions that balance the interests of different stakeholders. While SupTech can provide data-driven insights, more is needed to replace the judgment and discretion of human regulators.
- **Contextual understanding**: Regulators need to have a deep understanding of the regulatory context, including the legal and institutional framework, market dynamics, and industry practices. SupTech tools cannot replace this contextual understanding built through years of experience and training.

- **Legal and ethical considerations**: Regulators are responsible for ensuring that their decisions comply with legal and ethical standards, including fairness, transparency, and accountability. SupTech tools cannot make ethical judgments or ensure compliance with legal requirements.
- **Interpretation of results**: SupTech tools can provide data-driven insights, but interpreting results requires human judgment and expertise. Regulators need to be able to interpret and contextualize the results provided by SupTech tools to make informed decisions.

Moreover, SupTech is still new since its effectiveness has not been tested by a complete economic cycle. It is still being determined whether the limitations of new information technology will lead to new risks. Therefore, in the current financial regulation practice, SupTech can only provide preliminary and technical support for regulators to make judgments and decisions (Wang 2019).

7.3.4 Regulatory Arbitrage Concern

As mentioned above, the development of SupTech lags behind CompTech, and the problems caused by the uneven development have begun to highlight, mainly in SupTech's lagging of financial innovation and regulators' capacity restriction. Under the triple pressures of regulatory requirements, profit target, and cost constraints, financial institutions are naturally inclined to study and apply CompTech and introduce CompTech into the whole business management process to enhance compliance capabilities, reduce compliance costs, and ultimately achieve the goals of improving the operating model, improving operating efficiency and increasing profits. However, when all financial institutions begin to deeply study and apply CompTech, the financial regulators, due to constraints of factors such as staffing, capital, and technology, are developing slowly and need to catch up. Therefore, it is likely that financial institutions will be stimulated to use CompTech to look for regulatory loopholes, reduce the effectiveness of regulation, and even disregard the regulatory system, thus leading to new regulatory arbitrage (Zhao 2019).

7.3.5 Financial Inclusion Concern

FinTech is born with the gene of financial inclusion. Providing fast, low-cost, unsecured financial products and services plays a vital role in alleviating the difficulties of small and micro enterprises in obtaining financing and of disadvantaged groups in obtaining loans. With the development and application of CompTech, financial institutions have begun to use Big Data technology to collect personal information and behavioral data of customers and provide an accurate portrait of customers to provide grounds for risk control. Although using CompTech reduces manual intervention and improves the accuracy of risk control, the data collection dimensions and core algorithms of the risk control instruments based on Big Data technology are similar. When all financial institutions adopt the same or similar risk control instruments, some small and micro enterprises and disadvantaged groups will have no way to obtain financial services from any financial institution, which runs counter to the goal of financial inclusion (Zhao and Li 2020).

References

Monetary Authority of Singapore (16 Nov 2016) Fintech regulatory sandbox guideline
Monetary Authority of Singapore (Nov 2018) Principles to promote fairness, ethics, accountability and transparency (FEAT) in the use of artificial intelligence and data analytics in Singapore's financial sector
Monetary Authority of Singapore (Mar 2019) Consultation paper on proposed revisions to business continuity management guidelines
Sun G (2017) From FinTech to RegTech. Tsinghua Financ Rev (5)
Sun G (Apr 2019) Research and Practice in SupTech. Social Publishing House
Sun G (Oct 2019) China regulatory science and technology development report (2019). Social Publishing House
Sun G (Oct 2020) China regulatory science and technology development report (2020). Social Publishing House
Wang Q (2019) Analysis of several relational issues in the development of fintech. Financ Econ (5)
Zhao D (2019) Ability and inability of RegTech. Tsinghua Financ Rev (5)
Zhao D, Li X (2020) Research on financial supervision under the background of fintech on the perspective of RegTech, no 4. Zhejiang Finance
Zhao D, Li J (Apr 2021) Intelligent financial era. People's Daily Press

Chapter 8
SupTech Practices by Chinese Regulators

Introduction

While scientific and technological innovation injects new vitality into financial development, financial products become networked and digitalized, financial services increasingly fictitious, business boundaries gradually blurred, and the business environment increasingly open. As a result, different products and businesses are interrelated and interpenetrated, enhancing the availability of financial resources and making risk transmission break through the limitation of time and space. Moreover, it brings new challenges to financial regulation.

On the one hand, the cycle of technological iteration has shortened, and new business models and forms are emerging one after another. At the same time, detailed regulatory rules and risk control measures always appear only after long-term researches and explorations, let alone the formal legislation and legislative revisions. The above objectively leading to a lag in financial regulation.

On the other hand, as the hidden risks are more covert, complex, and spillover, it is easy to raise problems such as poor regulatory effects, low efficiency, and inconsistent standards if financial regulators only rely on non-standardized means such as window guidance and interview to carry out regulation. At the same time, in the face of pressing demands for innovation appeals and public demands, strict "one-size-fits-all" regulatory measures have failed to leave sufficient space for innovation and development and are likely to restrict the innovation capability of market players. Therefore, balancing innovation and risk prevention and fully releasing the vitality of financial innovation and development on the premise of maintaining financial stability has become an urgent problem that needs to be addressed for the financial sector's high-quality development (Zhao 2019).

In this context, the PBOC has carried out plenty of research and practice in SupTech, which is of great significance in accelerating the pace of digital transformation of financial regulation and establishing a modern financial regulatory system.

D. Zhao et al., *FinTech and SupTech in China*, Contributions to Finance and Accounting,
https://doi.org/10.1007/978-981-99-5173-4_8

8.1 SupTech Practices by PBOC Head Office and Branches

On May 18, 2020, the PBOC held the 2020 Science and Technology Work Videophone Conference in Beijing, where the science and technology work of the PBOC was required to follow Xi Jinping Thoughts on Socialism with Chinese Characteristics for a New Era, implement the decisions and arrangements of the CPC Central Committee and the State Council as well as the work requirements of the Party committees of the PBOC, and constantly improve the institutional mechanism of science and technology that is compatible with the modern central bank system. Furthermore, it was emphasized at the conference that scientific and technological support should be reinforced, a "Digital Central Bank" should be constructed, and the level of financial services and financial regulatory capacity should be enhanced. The overall objectives confirmed by the conference for PBOC's science and technology work task in the next stage are to strengthen the guidance for network security and informatization in the financial sector, to promote the implementation of cryptography applications and innovative development in the financial field, and to build a security barrier for the financial network.

Furthermore, the conference also called for promoting the high-quality development of FinTech, enhancing the ability of finance to serve the real economy, improving the application of LEI, and optimizing financial standards.

8.1.1 The PBOC Cloud

On July 23, 2021, the PBOC officially launched the bidding for cloud platform software, hardware, and support services for the cloud platform (Phase I) construction project. The software and hardware purchased for the project will be completed in Beijing and Shanghai for the "three centers" cloud infrastructure environment. The functions will cover IaaS, PaaS, unified cloud management service, and other main modules. The primary resources would be computing, storage, and network and platform services such as containers, databases, middleware, and security components. In addition, the cloud capabilities, such as integrated operation and maintenance, as well as measurement and billing, will be supported to achieve the pilot operation of some services of the PBOC on the cloud.

8.1.2 Second-Generation Credit Reference System

On January 17, 2020, The Credit Reference Center of the PBOC launched the project of switching to the second-generation credit reference system.

In recent years, China's economic and social development has put forward new requirements for increasing the adequate supply of credit and improving the level of credit information services. However, the development of FinTech has also provided technical support for further improvement of the service capability of credit information systems. To meet the needs of financial institutions and all sectors of society regarding credit information services and adapt to the development trend of FinTech, the Credit Reference Center of the PBOC launched the construction of the second-generation credit reference system promptly, which optimized and upgraded the credit reference system. Compared with the first-generation credit reference system, the second generation has been optimized and improved in information collection, product processing, technical framework, and security protection.

- Information contents are optimized and enriched, and the expandability, flexibility, and convenience of the information collection process are enhanced to reflect the credit status of information subjects more comprehensively and accurately.
- The display forms and generation mechanisms of credit reports are optimized, and the readability, adaptability, and convenience of credit reports are also enhanced.
- The system's technical framework is improved to support the rapid expansion of the system and resource optimization and to substantially enhance the efficiency of the information collection process and credit reference services.
- The system's security protection capabilities and the user identity and information transmission management are intensified to ensure credit information security.

8.1.3 PBOC Business Network of Collaborative Processing Platform

In November 2020, the Data Center of the PBOC, to establish an integrated and efficient information interaction platform, initiated bidding for the construction of a business network collaborative processing platform (the "Platform") for an agile and easy-to-use work coordination system, a unified and controllable resource-sharing center, and a flexible and rich data analysis tool to meet the relevant science and technology management needs. These can improve the level of science and technology management service, expand the way of horizontal and vertical coordination, eliminate the island of work information, and accurately monitor the performance of the Central Bank's obligations.

The overall requirements for the construction of the Platform are as follows: first, conduct localization implementation services based on the collaborative processing platform software ecology 9.0, and carry out the localization implementation of functional modules of the business network collaborative processing platform of the PBOC, such as application forms and processes configuration, etc.

Second, the Platform should be scalable and adopt clustering and load-balancing models and technologies such as componentized SOA. At all levels, it is required to be of scalability. Meanwhile, the application will not be affected by the growth of users. For upgrade, in principle, it is only necessary upon hardware.

Third, the Platform should have high reliability and availability and can achieve the goal of 7*24-hour operation.

Fourth, providing a rapid development platform that supports iterative and incremental rapid development, where technicians can initiate fast and convenient upgrades and maintenance. Fifthly, it should have high management ease of use and provide friendly, beautiful, and simple interfaces in operation, maintenance, configuration, monitoring, Etc.

8.1.4 SupTech Practices by PBOC Branches

8.1.4.1 "Canton Credit and Financing" by Guangzhou Branch

PBOC Guangzhou Branch builds a "Canton Credit and Financing" credit reporting platform to stabilize enterprises and safeguard employment. "Canton Credit and Financing," whose full name is Guangdong Provincial Credit Information and Financing Connection Platform for Micro, Small, and Medium-sized Enterprises, is an innovative local credit reporting platform established by the PBOC Guangzhou Branch, focusing on the financing difficulties and high financing costs of micro, small and medium-sized enterprises. In addition, this Platform aims to promote enterprise-related information sharing, develop the role of non-credit alternative data, creatively improve credit reporting services for micro, small, and medium-sized enterprises, provide financial institutions with practical information debiting decisions, and enhance the availability and coverage of financial services.

For the sake of protecting market players, the PBOC Guangzhou Branch has specially developed the functional module of "stabilizing enterprises and safeguarding employment" in "Canton Credit and Financing" to ensure the credit reporting platform works to help banks and enterprises connect precisely to promote the financial support within its jurisdiction to achieve positive results in stabilizing enterprises and safeguarding employment, and to achieve the job objective of "three targets and three highlights."

- Target Critical Enterprises and Highlight the Accuracy of Connection

Efforts should be made to, by relying on "Canton Credit and Financing," innovate, develop, and improve the functional module of stabilizing enterprises and guaranteeing employment, and strive to build an integrated connection interaction platform with a combination of list push, bank-enterprise connection, monitoring and analysis, information disclosure, experience promotion, policy publicity, interactive communication, etc. The list of critical enterprises provided by the departments of sector and information technology, departments of commerce, and development and reform commissions should be accurately transferred to banks, which should be urged to make offline visits and deliver feedback online. Hence a feedback mechanism of seamless online and offline connection will be formed. Under the premise of the authorization of enterprises, enterprises' credit information can, through "Canton Credit and Financing," assist banks in making credit decisions.

- Target Participants in the Inclusive Market and Highlight the Data-oriented Empowerment

"Canton Credit and Financing" uses FinTech, such as Big Data and Cloud Computing, to integrate information such as enterprises' business registration, tax, water, electricity payment, land resources, environmental protection, Etc. However, the chaotic information of micro, small, and medium-sized enterprises can be standardized, digitalized, and intellectualized to transform irregular information into a regular feasible one so as to build a bridge for information sharing between banks and enterprises. Therefore, it is essential to encourage financial institutions to apply massive data to serve the financing of micro, small and medium-sized enterprises, give play to the multiplication role of data elements on the efficiency of other elements, promote the transformation from data elements to production elements, and empower micro, small and medium-sized enterprises with financial services.

- Target Integrated Financial Services and Highlight the Positive Role of Credit Investigation

By establishing a model regulator as a critical aspect, the PBOC Guangzhou Branch earnestly practices the concept of "credit reporting for people" and enhances the convenience of credit investigation services. Furthermore, relying on the robust data in favor of the capacity of "Canton Credit and Financing," the Guangzhou Branch, also centering on financial service chains such as account opening, mortgage, and financing of market players, innovates and develops the enterprise account and settlement filing management system, real estate registration financial service system, foreign trade financing service system, and enterprise visiting management system, Etc. Meanwhile, the value of data has been dug more profound, the potential of data has been released, the integrated financial services in the field of micro, small and medium-sized enterprises, and people's livelihoods have been improved, and the capacity of credit reporting to benefit people and enterprises has been enhanced.

8.1.4.2 "Financial Inclusion in Villages" Platform by Chongqing Operations Office

PBOC Chongqing Operations Office built the "1 + 2 + N Inclusive Finance in Villages" online service platform and joined with financial institutions to promote online service platforms to reach villages and households, to achieve the provision of financial infrastructure to villages, public services to households and digital inclusion to people.

- Form a Comprehensive Service Platform of Inclusive Finance

It is essential to integrate various financial information resources and QR codes of eight functional sections, including the rural comprehensive financial service station, financial consumer protection station, and financial knowledge publicity station. Therefore, by scanning the QR codes, farmers can reach financial knowledge, inquire about financial services, select financial products, and get financial consulting, all through codes. In the process, business handling codes can be improved.

- Build a Financial Inclusion Supply and Demand Docking Platform

It is essential to establish an inclusive finance product supermarket to display the supply information of inclusive finance credit products and wealth management products and establish an "agriculture, rural areas, and farmers" financial demand center to display the financial demand information of various "agriculture, rural areas, and farmers" entities to achieve the accurate peer-to-peer matching between the supply and demand of inclusive finance.

- Construct a Big Data Platform for Inclusive Finance

It is significant to use Big Data, Cloud Computing, and other digital technologies for establishing a Big Data center of inclusive finance to villages while collecting multi-dimensional data on the effectiveness of inclusive financial services in supporting rural revitalization, such as credit support for industrial development, green financial synergy and protection of farmers' financial consumer rights and interests. In the meantime, comprehensively and systematically monitor and evaluate the development level of inclusive finance of all regional administrative villages to support better financial services to help rural revitalization.

8.1.4.3 Technology-Driven Regulation of Credit Investigation by Changchun Sub-branch

In recent years, the PBOC Changchun Central Sub-branch has earnestly explored the application of science and technology to constantly promote the electrification and standardization of credit inquiry, supervision, and publicity and effectively improve the level of regulation upon credit investigation services.

- Promote the front-end system for credit inquiry and realize electronic counter inquiries for credit information

The Changchun Central Sub-branch of the PBOC organizes establishing and promoting the front-end system for a credit inquiry, realizes the electronic classification management of inquiry files, and ensures that each credit inquiry is subject to examination and approval and complete vital documents. The system introduces infrared face comparison technology to verify the identity of an inquiry user to avoid the risk of fraudulent use by the user and false checking of credit reports. Meanwhile, the system will record and trace the log-in time, log-out time, operations of the users, and other information. It will enable inquiry according to different dimensions (time interval, user name, Etc.) to ensure that the behaviors of the users are traceable. Furthermore, the system will, in light of the actual business, conduct continuous monitoring of abnormal situations such as inquiries at an unconventional time, increasing the number of inquiries, and inquiries in other places through optimizing the threshold value calculation model and reasonably setting monitoring indicators for the sake of realizing early warning, early detection, and early handling.

- Build an off-site supervision system for credit information services and intensify the compliance management of the agencies with access to credit information

The Changchun Central Sub-branch of the PBOC has, in light of the problems existing in the compliance management of credit information services in Jilin Province, such as a large number of managed objects, seldom management personnel, on-site supervision lagging, and insufficient off-site supervision measures. After in-depth study and analysis, an off-site supervision system has been established for credit information services. The system has six functions: data collection, monitoring, early warning, evaluation management, task management, pre-positioned takeover, and inquiry statistics, respectively. Based on the data collected from the agencies with access to credit information, the system can promptly detect and locate credit risks by relying on the risk early warning model. The work efficiency and fairness of credit information evaluation will be improved by automatically generating supervision and evaluation reports according to the predefined rules. Furthermore, the system will automatically issue off-site inspection tasks. The institutions subject to the inspection will deliver their detailed electronic archives within a prescribed time limit based on the retrieved list. The method of inspection conducted by this system is very similar to that of on-site inspection and can promote the compliance of all entities in terms of credit information services.

- Develop a navigation program for credit inquiry outlets to facilitate the public's access to credit information services

The Changchun Central Sub-branch of the PBOC has actively developed and launched the "Map Navigation for Self-service Inquiry Outlets in Jilin Province" Program to provide the public with more intuitive and convenient credit inquiry services. The Program contains information on all outlets placing self-service inquiry equipment for credit information services in Jilin Province. It updates the information of such outlets promptly according to the actual situation to ensure the display of the most up-to-date and complete information about the credit inquiry outlets in Jilin Province. The Program relies on the WeChat platform, where the public may select the nearest credit inquiry outlets according to the place where they belong. Meanwhile, the Program is seamlessly linked with users' self-owned map software on mobile phones. It can jump to the map APPs on mobile phones in the light of users' needs, to automatically locate and navigate to the intended credit inquiry outlets, and to facilitate faster and more convenient self-service inquiries for the public.

8.1.4.4 Credit Information Platform for Financial Inclusion by Ningbo Sub-branch

To effectively alleviate the information asymmetry between banks and enterprises as well as banks and farmers, provide an efficient connection channel for information inquiry, client searching, risk warning, and financing, and reduce both credit trading costs and risks of financial institutions for inclusive finance services. However, the credit information service platform for inclusive finance, which is guided by the Ningbo Central Sub-branch of the PBOC and constructed by the Ningbo Fund Clearing Center, has been officially launched since November 2018. In November 2019, after Ningbo was approved as a national-level pilot inclusive finance reform zone, the Platform was vigorously promoted as an essential infrastructure for the pilot inclusive finance reform zone. The iterative upgrading of version 2.0 of the Platform has been launched based on the continuation of the original function points of the Platform, and the Platform has been officially launched for operation since December 2020. The main functions and effects of the Platform are as follows:

- First, mass information has been integrated and shared platform-based to achieve full coverage of information subjects. The channels for sharing public Big Data resources and public credit information in Ningbo have been unblocked. Furthermore, an integrated data collection platform has been established to achieve real-time data retrieval from the Bureau of Natural Resources and Planning. It has been connected with the provincial "guarantee loan registration system" and "enterprise credit information platform," as well as the "Xinyidai" platform of the National Development and Reform Commission to achieve the interconnection of credit information.
- Second, the multi-dimensional portrait of users' characteristics has generated nearly 10,000 information inquiries per day. The Platform has introduced Big Data analysis methods, and machine learning modes, continuously improved the evaluation model, and launched personalized information inquiry services such as real estate instant inquiry, recommendation of enterprises in the cultivation pool, enterprise genealogy relationship, and enterprise risk warning to provide a multi-dimensional portrait of customers. Financial institutions have generally regarded the inquiry application of the Platform as a vital link in the business expansion and risk management of inclusive finance.
- Third, precise financing docking services have been provided with a success rate of nearly 50%. The Platform has connected the supply and demand sides and developed the "Ningbo inclusive loan" APP to facilitate the demand for financing services. In addition, the Platform has summarized the details of various financial products of financial institutions, as well as various policies and measures and notable activities of the national, provincial, and municipal governments and financial regulators, effectively supporting the precise implementation of the expansion of initial borrowers, extension loans, and credit loan policies. Meanwhile, the Platform provides services such as financing applications and demand registration. Enterprises can realize a two-way choice between the supply and

demand of funds by submitting targeted or public financing demand online. For qualified enterprises, loans should be granted in the most extensive range and fastest speed.

- Fourth, whole-process institutional technology protection has been implemented to ensure the information security of the Platform. Given the requirements of information protection and data security, it is vital to intensify the face recognition and identity verification of the Platform and develop the measures for information management upon the Platform. It is also significant to regulate the collection, sorting, query, and application of the information in the whole field of government, business and finance, dispute handling, and other matters, and ensure that all data processing activities comply with the laws and regulations. Meanwhile, the platform subjects should be respectively deployed on the financial MAN, the government extranet, and the internet. Furthermore, each network has different functions and information categories. Such links as information collection, query and application, and dispute handling constitute a complete business process to meet the needs of different groups. Simultaneously physical isolation should be implemented between each network to prevent attacks, illegal visits, and leakage risks from the internet. At last, data desensitization and privileged access measures are adopted to control the scope of persons aware of the information strictly.

8.2 Pilot Supervision on FinTech Innovation by the PBOC

In December 2019, with the support of the PBOC, Beijing took the lead in launching the pilot supervision for FinTech innovations. Information disclosure, an announcement of statements, joint supervision, and other flexible management methods are applied to explore an inclusive and prudent FinTech innovation regulatory mechanism.

In January 2020, the PBOC Operations Office (Beijing) organized a meeting in Beijing to launch the pilot supervision of Fintech innovation. In the same month, Beijing announced the regulatory pilot applications of Fintech innovation (the first batch in 2020).

In April 2020, the PBOC announced that it would expand the innovative Fintech regulatory pilots in six cities (districts): Shanghai, Chongqing, Shenzhen, Xiong'an New Area, Hangzhou, and Suzhou. After that, in June 2020, Beijing launched the second batch of supervision pilots of Fintech innovation.

In July 2020, Shanghai and Shenzhen launched the first batch of regulatory pilots of Fintech innovation and made the same public. In August 2020, Xiong'an New Area, Chongqing, Suzhou, Hangzhou, Guangzhou, and Chengdu launched the first batch of regulatory pilots of Fintech innovation.

In October 2020, the White Paper on China's Regulation of Fintech Innovation was officially released.

Timeline	Regulatory Pilot Project
December	On December 5, 2019, the PBOC announced it would favor Beijing taking the lead in conducting innovative Fintech regulatory pilots.
January	On January 14, 2020, Beijing launched the first batch of innovative Fintech regulatory pilots.
April	On April 27, 2020, the PBOC announced that it would expand the innovative Fintech regulatory pilots in six cities (districts): Shanghai, Chongqing, Shenzhen, Xiong'an New Area, Hangzhou, and Suzhou.
June	In June (2020). Beijing launched the second batch of innovative Fintech regulatory pilots.
July	On July 31, 2020, Shanghai launched the first batch of innovative Fintech regulatory pilots. On July 20, 2020, Shenzhen launched the first batch of innovative Fintech regulatory pilots.
August	On August 7, 2020, Chongqing launched the first batch of innovative Fintech regulatory pilots. On August 14, 2020, Xiong'an New Area, Hangzhou, and Suzhou launched the first batch of innovative Fintech regulatory pilots. On August 24, 2020, Canton and Chengdu launched the first batch of innovative Fintech regulatory pilots.
October	On October 22, 2020, the *White Paper on China's Regulation upon Fintech Innovation* was officially released.
December	On December 25, 2020, Beijing launched the third batch of innovative Fintech regulatory pilots. On December 31, 2020, Shanghai launched the second batch of innovative Fintech regulatory pilots.

Fig. 8.1 China's timeline of the regulatory application pilots

At the end of December 2020, Beijing and Shanghai announced the second and the third batches of the innovative regulatory pilots, respectively. So far, in 2020, a total of 70 innovative regulatory pilots have been launched in nine regions in China (Fig. 8.1).

8.2.1 Main Measures Adopted by the Regulatory Pilots

The regulatory pilots, through flexible methods such as information disclosure and public supervision, in combination with the rigid bottom lines in terms of business compliance, technology security, and risk controllability, create a moderately relaxed development environment for FinTech innovation, reserve sufficient development space for precious Fintech innovation, effectively empowering the application of innovative technologies, releasing the value of data elements, and promoting the stable and far-reaching development of Fintech in China on the road of innovative development.

8.2.1.1 Build a Diversified Collaborative Governance System

The pilot programs, based on strengthening the internal control management of financial market participants and implementing government supervision, fully mobilize the enthusiasm of all social participants, introduce diversified forces to participate in Fintech governance, and continuously promote the orderly implementation of various regulatory policies with the leading government departments. Self-disciplinary organizations should exert a positive effect as bridges and ties to cooperate in policy publicity and implementation. Also, it is available for the public to participate in the whole-process supervision through various channels and methods. Financial operators should fulfill their primary responsibilities and intensify their internal control of risks and capacity for self-discipline. With the efforts of various subjects, a four-in-one defensive line for the regulation of Fintech innovation, which includes institutional autonomy, public supervision, sector self-discipline, and government supervision, should be formed.

8.2.1.2 Establish a Lifecycle Innovation Management Mechanism

The pilot programs incorporate the whole-process innovation into the scope of regulation by establishing a management mechanism covering the product design, risk prevention and control, and supervision and management of Fintech innovation. Before the innovation, players in innovation are guided to establish and improve the risk prevention and consumer protection mechanism through project counseling, publicity, public supervision, and other methods. During the innovation, the operation of innovative applications should be continuously and dynamically monitored by the SupTech measures, while risk hazards should be dynamically tracked and resolved. However, safety control of the whole-process innovation should be strengthened. After the innovation, various complaint channels, including the market participants and self-regulatory organizations, should be established, with supporting punishment measures such as interviews, warnings, and a compulsory withdrawal system to initiate supervision and management properly.

8.2.1.3 Create a Tolerable Space for Errors in the Innovation

The concept of flexible regulation should be fully practiced to build a testing space with the "trial and error" function, based on strictly preventing innovation risks from spilling over, to support innovative entities to complete business chain practice and testing of theoretical prototypes, technology selection and business models of innovative application in a realistic market environment, timely discover and remedy potential risks, effectively verify the innovative value, and create an innovational atmosphere of "mistakes tolerance, mistakes timely discover, and mistakes rapid correction." Furthermore, not only should prudential regulation be strengthened to avoid systemic financial risks, but regulatory inclusiveness should be enhanced to fully reserve development space for new business forms and models and effectively release the driving force of financial innovation development.

8.2.1.4 Build Line of Defense for the Consumer Protection

In this context, the people-centered development concept should be upheld. It is assumed that consumers' capital allocation rights, information security rights, and the right to know should be effectively protected. Financial consumers should be informed, through innovative application publicity and self-declaration mechanism, to comprehensively understand the functional substance, potential risks, and compensation measures of innovative products so that the right to know and the right to make independent choices can be safeguarded. Efforts should also be made to urge innovative entities to intensify security management of data lifecycle, strictly prevent data leakage, tampering, damage, and improper application, and ensure the safety of consumer information. The methods for determining risk liability should be specified, compensation channels should be established, and compensation measures such as risk provisions and insurance plans should be supported to protect the property safety of consumers effectively. A multi-level consumer complaint and recommendation mechanism, including innovative entities, industry associations, and regulators, should be set to effectively protect consumers' right to supervision and right of recommendation.

8.2.1.5 Build Incubation Carriers for Scientific and Technological Achievements

On the one hand, professional counseling teams should be organized to provide "one-to-one" professional regulation and counseling services, to guide innovative entities to maintain integrity, innovation effectively, and the safe of applications, and to accelerate the cultivation of quality products and services that both meet market needs and regulatory requirements. On the other hand, through revealing the advantages of the scaled-down real scenario, i.e., "one end connects the market, one end connects the government, and one end connects the users," a platform for production-use connection, government-enterprise collaboration, and supply-demand matching should be established to deeply activate innovative ingredients and resources, and reduce the cost of technological innovation. Also, it is critical to shorten the innovation incubation cycle and enhance the efficiency of transformation and application of technological innovation achievements to foster fertile soil for the growth of Fintech innovation (Sun 2019a).

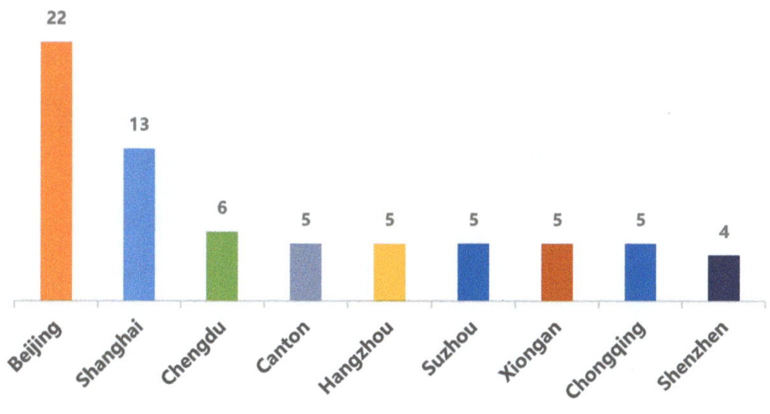

Fig. 8.2 Fintech innovative application pilots in China

8.2.2 *Implementation Status of Pilot Supervisions*

As of the end of 2020, in China, 70 innovative application projects for the benefit of the people and enterprises had been launched in nine regions, and remarkable results had been achieved in the innovative FinTech regulatory pilots.

8.2.2.1 Regional Distribution

From the perspective of regional distribution, by 2020, among the nine pilot regions, Beijing had launched three batches of 22 projects (31%), with apparent leading status, followed by Shanghai, with two batches of 13 projects (19%) launched. On the other hand, Chengdu had launched a batch of 6 projects (9%), Guangzhou, Hangzhou, Suzhou, Xiong'an, Chongqing, and other regions launched a batch of 5 projects (7%), and Shenzhen launched a batch of 4 projects (6%) (Fig. 8.2).

8.2.2.2 Type Distribution of Innovative Entities

By 2020, on the whole, a total of 106 institutions across China had participated in the pilot programs. Among them, 68 are financial institutions (accounting for 64%), and 38 are technology companies (accounting for 36%).

Among the financial institutions, banking institutions play a leading role, with 54 institutions participating, led by large state-owned banks such as the Industrial and Commercial Bank of China, Agricultural Bank of China, China Construction Bank, and Bank of Communications. In addition, joint-stock banks such as Shanghai Pudong Development Bank, China Minsheng Bank, Ping An Bank, and local commercial banks such as Bank of Shanghai and Bank of Chongqing also actively participate. In addition, there are seven non-banking payment institutions,

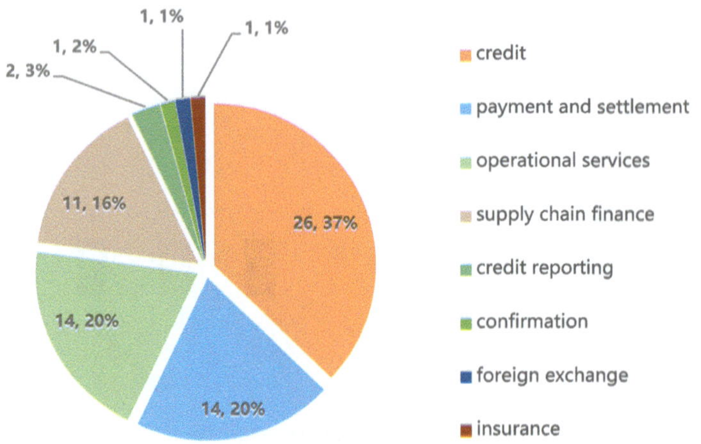

Fig. 8.3 Distribution map of innovative application scenarios

four credit reporting agencies (including one personal credit reporting agency and three corporate credit reporting filing agencies), two insurance companies, and one liquidation organization. For example, ICBC Technology, CCB FinTech, and CIB Fintech; telecommunication operators and relevant enterprises, such as China Telecom System Integration, China Mobile Information Technology, and Shanghai Ideal Information; internet companies and relevant organizations, such as JD Finance, DuXMan, and Tencent Cloud, and; technical service providers in various fields, such as scientific research institutes, logistics, electric power, and tax planning are also included.

8.2.2.3 Distribution of Application Scenarios

From the perspective of application scenarios, among the 70 innovative FinTech application projects, traditional financing credit scenarios account for the highest proportion of 26, the proportion of which is 37%; there are 14 scenarios of payment and settlement and 14 scenarios in operational services respectively, totally accounting for 20%; there are 11 scenarios of supply chain finance, which occupy 16%; there are two scenarios of credit reporting, accounting for 3%; and there are one scenario of insurance, foreign exchange, and confirmation respectively, totally accounting for 1% (Fig. 8.3).

8.2.2.4 Distribution of Key Underlying Technologies of SupTech

Overall, the pilot program for the supervision of FinTech innovation focuses on three technologies: Big Data, AI, and Blockchain, and many projects involve several vital technologies. Among them, 54 projects involve Big Data, 49 involve AI, and 24

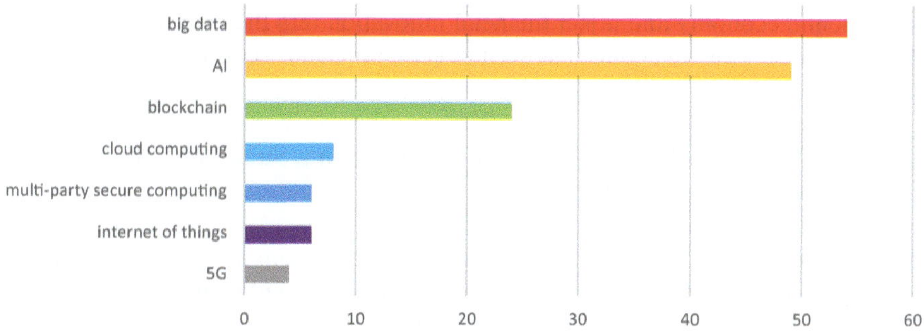

Fig. 8.4 Distribution of key underlying technologies for innovative application

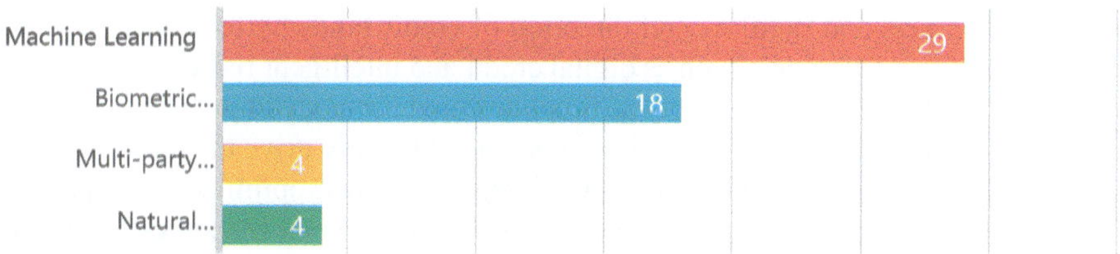

Fig. 8.5 Application distribution of AI technologies

involve Blockchain. The numbers of projects involving Cloud Computing, secure multi-party computing, Internet of Things, and 5G are eight, six, six, and four, respectively (Fig. 8.4).

Among them, AI technologies involve the most significant number of categories with the most diversified applications. Machine learning (including deep learning, neural network, etc.) and biometric recognition (including image recognition, speech recognition, etc.) constitute the leading technologies, of which 29 involve machine learning and 18 involve biometric recognition. It is followed by four projects, each of multi-party data learning and natural language processing (Fig. 8.5).

8.2.2.5 Achievements of the Regulatory Pilot

The pilot programs, centering on China's major development strategies, guide financial institutions and technology companies to make appropriate applications of data and technical methods, strengthening the application of innovative technologies, alleviating the financing problems of small and micro enterprises, get through the "last mile" of inclusive finance, and helping the implementation of the rural revitalization strategy as the driving force. In addition, however, a series of application projects for benefiting the people and enterprises as well as upholding the integrity and making innovation is launched to provide "precision irrigation" financial service support for the authentic economy and inject financial innovation into the overall promotion of epidemic prevention and control as well as economic and social development.

8.2.2.6 Alleviating the Financing Difficulties Facing Small and Micro Private Enterprises

The pilot programs focus on empowering finance to benefit people and enterprises through modern information technologies. The use of Cloud Computing, Big Data, AI, and other information technologies should be effectively explored to intensify the integrated application of data in finance and government affairs, sector and commerce, power, and other fields for providing "precision irrigation" financial services for the real economy. The pilot programs also grasp the credit status of enterprises' assets and the flow and direction of credit funds by technical and data methods, create new models such as digital credit and intelligent risk control, reduce reliance on collaterals, and enhance the timeliness and accuracy of pricing for current assets and intangible assets. In addition, it is crucial to fully drive the multiplication effect of data elements on the efficiency of other elements, optimize the supply of funds for supply chains, and guide the allocation of financial resources to critical fields and vulnerable segments of economic and social development. Moreover, it is also critical to provide enterprises that resume work and production and small and micro private enterprises with non-contact financing services at lower rates, on a larger scale, and more intelligent for the sake of helping achieve the precision irrigation of finance into the practical economy.

For example, China UnionPay, the Pudong Development Bank, and the Bank of Shanghai have jointly built a Blockchain-based integrated application platform for financial and government data in Shanghai to assist in solving the problems of difficulty and high cost of financing for small and micro enterprises. Additionally, Titanion Intelligent Technology (Suzhou) Co., Ltd., and Bank of Suzhou Co., Ltd. provide financial institutions with the inquiry, analysis, and visualization functions for the integration of upstream and downstream information of supply chains and the sector knowledge base, which are mainly applied in the scenarios of credit loan for small and medium enterprises in the upstream and downstream of supply chains.

8.2.2.7 Improving Financial Services for the Convenience and Benefit of People

The pilot programs have used technological methods such as image recognition, voice recognition, and edge computing to intensify users' digital cognition, create situational perceptive financial services in combination with users' preferences, and promote the in-depth coupling of finance with scenes such as necessities, food, housing and transportation, and medical education. In the meantime, it is considered that should achieve a transparent allocation of funds and amounts, intelligent services at bank outlets and integrated application of credit information, and provide more comprehensive, more considerate, and more heartwarming financial products and services for different customer groups including the elderly, the disabled, residents in remote areas and ethnic minorities. For example, the Credit Card Center of CITIC Bank develops an intelligent digital card issuance mode featuring "intelligent manual face-to-face signing + AI image recognition," which realizes the whole-process online handling of credit card issuance. As a result, it provides customers with safe, convenient, intelligent, and efficient credit card services. In addition, the Bank of Chengdu and Chongqing Rural Commercial Bank launched intelligent bank customer service supporting the dialects of Sichuan and Chongqing to provide more convenient inclusive financial services for different social groups, predominantly middle-aged, elderly customers.

8.2.2.8 Assisting in the Implementation of the Rural Revitalization Strategy

Considering the pain points and difficulties in the development of agriculture, rural areas, and farmers, pilot programs try to explore the use of satellite remote sensing, Big Data, the internet of things, a reliable execution environment, and other new generation of information technology, optimize agriculture-related financial services benefiting farmers in light of local conditions, and create digital financial products suitable for rural areas. Pilot programs also make use of technology to bridge the "digital gap" in rural areas, solve the shortage of agricultural funds, promote the penetration and inclusive development of rural finance, and effectively enhance the rural finance carrying capacity, the modernization of the agricultural sector and the availability of financial services for farmers. For instance, online commercial banks extend inclusive finance to traditional agriculture based on satellite remote sensing and AI technology, serve vast stretches of farmland, and help revitalize the rural sector. However, the Rural Commercial Banks in Shangtong and Chengdu, Sichuan province, because of the problem that farmers hardly provide valid credit data for banks due to seldom financial activities, launched the rural finance service system to benefit the farmers, which, by integrating the government data of various parties and build the farmer credit information and data system, solves the problem of difficulty and high cost of financing in rural areas, also helps with the development of local agriculture, rural areas, and farmers.

8.2.2.9 Strengthening the Capacity for Technical Prevention of Financial Risks

Pilot programs actively explore the use of secure multi-party computing, knowledge atlas, privacy computing, and other technologies, initiate safe and efficient integration and sharing of data of all parties based on a determined domain, build a risk prevention and control system, enhance the overall risk control level of financial institutions, and intensify the application of CompTech in the financial sector. For example, the

Bank of Communications, through secure multi-party computing and knowledge atlas technology, integrates its internal data with government, telecommunications, and other external data, breaks the existing data barrier, accurately identifies the complex relationship chains and fraud risks behind enterprise clusters, and builds a safe and efficient risk control platform. In addition, the State Grid Credit Reference Co., Ltd., relying on Big Data technologies such as neural network algorithm and time series analysis algorithm, and based on the underlying power Big Data, builds a whole-process online management platform for credit risks so that power data can be reasonably applied to all sections of bank credit business, to provide a complete solution for credit risk control (Sun 2020).

8.3 Research on the Construction of the SupTech System in China

8.3.1 Main Tasks for the Construction of China's SupTech System

To implement the requirements of "improving the financial regulatory system and keeping the bottom line of non-occurrence of systematic financial risks" set out at the 19th National Congress of the CPC, it is of great practical significance to intensify the construction of the SupTech system, and promoting the application of SupTech is the main task for future regulatory informatization work.

Currently, China has a foundation and conditions to initiate the construction of the SupTech system. Firstly, supervision informatization has achieved success. In addition, the central regulatory information platform has provided a data foundation. However, many entities have explored and looked forward on Big Data and machine learning. Secondly, the constant maturity and implementation of Big Data, Cloud Computing, and other technologies have provided the technical foundation. The successful application of various AI algorithms has provided advanced examples. Therefore, constructing the SupTech system is an important work that is technically feasible and urgently needed. The main tasks in constructing a SupTech system should include the following.

8.3.1.1 Improve Macro-Prudential Regulation and Prevent Systemic Financial Risks

FinTech is a double-edged sword. The application of AI and other new technologies in the financial sector will make the risk transmission paths more complicated, the flow of funds more frequent, and the violation of laws and regulations more concealed, which will harm the stable operation of the financial market. It requires the regulators to use technical methods more rationally and effectively to take a further step forward, forming early predictions and responses, improving the identification and monitoring of new market operations, maintaining the stable operation of the financial market, strengthening the capacity to prevent systematic financial risks, and better serving the practical economy.

8.3.1.2 Promote Micro-Prudential Regulation

The construction of the SupTech system can enhance the prudential regulation level of China's regulators to make the formulation of rules more scientific and the assessment system more objective. In particular, the application of Big Data, AI, and other advanced technologies can enable the timely and effective discovery and analysis of abnormal transactions, insider trading, market manipulation, fraudulent disclosure of information, and other activities, conduct more efficient regulation of all types of market players and promote the healthy and orderly development of all types of market players.

8.3.1.3 Enrich Technical Methods for Financial Consumer Protection

On the one hand, using technological methods for regulation can enhance the effectiveness of risk warnings. However, compared with traditional methods, it can provide more rapid and comprehensive reports on the capital market dynamics and detect abnormal market movements and other problems in time. On the other hand, by applying new technologies, regulatory measures can be continuously enriched, while regulatory capabilities and effectiveness can be enhanced. The sharing of cross-market monitoring information can be used to crack down on illegal securities institutions, penalize illegal activities, and effectively protect small and medium investors' legitimate rights and interests.

8.3.1.4 Enhance Regulatory Efficiency and Rationality

Combining modern information technology with regulation can not only effectively enhance the supervising and monitoring capacity and business service capacity of financial regulators but also able to optimize and transform the existing supervision and regulatory processes with new technologies, to promote the reform of financial regulatory concepts and regulatory methods, and the in-depth integration of technology and business. It is also necessary to further intensify the regulatory inspection and law enforcement capabilities, to enhance regulatory efficiency in all aspects before, during, and after the event, and to provide more comprehensive, scientific, and objective decision-making support for financial regulators.

While promoting the development SupTech, China follows the general principles of "led by science and technology and driven by demand; built together and shared, multi-party collaboration; overall planning and continuous promotion; enhancement of capacity and innovation of mechanism," and establishes an integrated technology-based and intelligent service platform for financial regulation of the capital market.

The meaning of leading by science and technology while driving by demand refers to the use of advanced science and technology to guide the regulation, promote the innovation of regulatory models, and comprehensively analyze and understand the actual needs and pain points of various departments and institutions, to achieve the targeted development of SupTech. However, the definition of building together and sharing, insisting on multi-party collaboration, refers to the implementation model that unifies various departments and institutions to build the Big Data platform jointly. In the work of SupTech, various parties should cooperate, support each other, and jointly use the Big Data platform to solve practical regulatory problems. Overall planning and continuous promotion refer to the management approach that the FinTech Committee of the PBOC should, under the unified leadership and organization of the Financial Stability and Development Committee of the State Council, take the lead in planning and building all aspects of the SupTech system, and should, in light of business needs, promote the building of the entire Platform and application services in phases and at different levels. Enhancement of capacity and innovation of mechanism refers to the establishment of a new SupTech system, mechanism, and capacity through the establishment of a Big Data platform and a diversified analysis center for promoting the innovation of financial regulation model, improving the efficiency of financial services to the real economy, and achieving the full inclusion of financial risk regulation in the capital market.

Efforts upon SupTech should fully comply with the above general construction principles and should further achieve the integration of various data resources under an overall layout planning to serve various routine regulatory work better, comprehensively enhance the intellectual level of financial regulation, and promote the reform of financial regulation concepts and regulatory methods. Also, the security and expansion ability should be taken into account when developing the Platform to ensure that the collection and use of information and data and the application of new technologies will be realized under a secure technical system, with full consideration given to the needs of rapid development of capital market business.

In China, the development path of SupTech is based on the actual situation of China's financial market. Based on strengthening electronic and networked regulation, we should provide regulators with comprehensive and accurate data and analysis services through Big Data, Cloud Computing, AI, Etc., to further meet the relevant needs of financial regulation and achieve the following three goals:

- Improve the construction of various infrastructures and central regulation information platforms and achieving the interconnection of business processes and the comprehensive sharing of data to form a comprehensive and whole-process support for regulation.
- Actively apply Big Data, Cloud Computing, and other technological means to initiate real-time data collection, real-time data calculation, and real-time data analysis to achieve real-time monitoring of market operations, improve the capability of monitoring market risks and identifying abnormal transactions, and

early detect and timely dispose of various securities and futures illegalities and irregularities.

- Explore the use of AI technologies, including machine learning algorithms, deep learning algorithms, and data mining, to provide financial regulation with intelligent applications and services to optimize various regulatory work models such as ex-ante examination, interim monitoring, and ex-post investigation, and punishment, to improve the capability and intelligence of self-detection of problems, and to promote innovation in financial regulation models.

8.3.2 Establishment of China's SupTech Framework

The core of China's SupTech framework is establishing an efficiently operated regulatory Big Data platform and comprehensively using data analysis technologies, such as electronic warning, statistical analysis, and data mining, to conduct real-time monitoring, historical analysis, and investigation. Meanwhile, China's SupTech system will assist regulatory personnel in conducting a panoramic analysis of market participants and real-time monitoring of the overall market conditions, detect suspected insider trading timely, market manipulation and other illegalities and irregularities, fulfill regulatory duties, and safeguard trading orders of the market. Therefore, the overall framework for the development of China's SupTech system should be as follows:

- Establish a logically integrated regulatory Big Data platform. The Big Data platform on supervision is the core of the SupTech system. The Platform can carry internal transaction, disclosure, and regulatory data from different regulatory systems and various external data resources and be integrated and unified in logic to provide essential data support for various data analyses and applications by the upper management. Regulatory Big Data platforms can apply virtualization or container technology to achieve the unified management of computing, memory, storage, network, etc. A proprietary cloud platform can also be logically constructed. Also, a distributed architecture is used to collect, store, compute, and manage mass data. At the same time, we may provide deep learning, graph analysis, other general algorithms and models, and tools such as voice recognition and image recognition for upper analysis centers (Fu and Liu 2018).
- Establish multiple flexible and intelligent data analysis centers. Several data analysis centers are suggested to set up the business requirements of different regulatory areas under unified planning by the central bank. Each analysis center can apply the mass of data in the Big Data platform to conduct data analysis and processing according to the requirements of different regulatory areas.
- Provide standardized and diverse professional analysis services. Each analysis center can provide one or more business analysis services in a single regulatory area, with no duplication of essential services between the analysis centers. The PBOC may also organize to provide some standardized services, such as panoramic portrait services, financial analysis services, Etc. Services requiring

special data, special algorithms, or special fields can be handed over to an analysis center or a dispatched agency for personalized construction.

- Form good coordination with regard to FinTech regulation and SupTech development among financial regulators, including the PBOC, the CSRC, the CBIRC, etc. Various business departments require specialized data analysis services, and in technical implementation, the entry of service requests is integrated into the central regulatory information platform. The analysis results of each analysis center will be provided to the application systems of different regulatory information platforms in the form of function modules or data services, where they will be displayed and subsequently processed and used, and served by various business departments. Therefore, the Big Data platform mainly completes real-time monitoring and data analysis services, and the central regulatory information platform mainly completes workflow management and day-to-day regulatory cooperation. The regulatory Big Data platform and central regulatory information platform are closely connected and effectively linked to each other, constituting a unified whole.

Regarding construction, the infrastructure layer is the lowest layer of the Big Data platform and the foundation of the entire Big Data platform. The infrastructure includes an advanced physical facility, an efficient network transmission system, and a unified resource management system.

8.3.2.1 Building Advanced Physical Facility

- Establishing server cluster

The architecture of a Big Data platform requires robust scalability. Therefore, a server cluster needs to be built. The use of a general X86 server cluster can meet the hardware requirements of the server, coupled with the convenient and flexible cluster expansion function, which will significantly reduce the procurement cost of the server. At the same time, the plug-and-play deployment of the universal server is simple, which makes the maintenance and replacement of failed components more convenient, and reduces the maintenance burden. In the configuration of the server, the number of cores of the server CPU directly affects the parallel processing ability of the system. Hence a CPU with a high number of cores should be used as far as possible to ensure the parallel processing ability of the system. The throughput of Big Data computation is large, so the system memory is high, and the amount of memory needs to be increased on the server.

- Establishing an efficient network transmission system

The Big Data cluster contains massive data, and internal data exchanges are frequent. Therefore, high network bandwidth is required. Consequently, in terms of network construction, special Ethernet lines with higher bandwidth should be applied, and dual network card links for the server should be aggregated to improve the reliability and bandwidth of the network. Furthermore, to fully release the processing ability of the Big Data platform, high-end exchangers should be selected as far as possible. Meanwhile, dual redundancy should be adopted in the exchangers to ensure the reliability of the network and improve the bandwidth.

- Establishing a stable storage system

The Big Data platform cluster has features such as high availability and stability at the software level. Furthermore, in terms of storage selection, internal hard disks can be used to meet the requirements of high availability and stability, and the storage expandability can be completed by the Big Data platform automatically through allocation by increasing nodes.

8.3.2.2 Building a Secure Network Architecture

Based on the sensitivity of various data, the network architecture can be mainly divided into the secret-involved intranet with a security level of "confidential," the securities and networking system with a higher security level, and the external internet. Therefore, the security characteristics of three different security levels should be considered when considering the network architecture design of the Big Data platform and fully meet the security requirements of the financial regulation on the network through the use of special lines, physical isolation, and logical isolation.

- Secret-involved intranet

The secret-involved intranet refers to some secret-involved data of the regulators. The main service objects are the government organs and local offices of the State Council, and some of the secret-involved intranet terminals. Therefore, it is designed to ensure high data security by directly applying special lines and one-way gateways to isolate the network from the outside world physically.

- Internet

Utilize the internet to achieve smooth communication with the external network and adopt various access control measures to ensure data security.

8.3.2.3 Building a Unified Resource Management System

The Big Data platform needs a unified resource management system to manage all kinds of bottom software and hardware resources. Therefore, a unified resource management system should be established to implement multi-tenant resource quota management, to achieve unified management of resources, elastic sharing, and isolation of resources and data.

- Unified management for promoting the manageability of the system

The unified resource management platform uniformly manages the CPU, memory, storage, network, and other resources. However, simultaneously, it breaks through the limitation of single-machine management while making the resource management move from single-machine management to cluster management and run through the whole life cycle of the use of service resources.

- Elastic sharing of resources for improving the utilization of resources

The flexible deployment and elastic scalability of the unified resources enable the system resources to be shared between different tenants, which will significantly improve the utilization of resources.

- Isolation for guaranteeing the quality and security of services

Generally, data, computation, and application are isolated perfectly within several resources. Therefore, it is vital that isolating different services can guarantee the quality and security of services.

8.3.2.4 Building a Stable Data Transmission System

The first consideration is the transmission from the confidential intranet to the external network. The data of the confidential intranet involve confidential information. Due to the physical isolation characteristics of the confidential intranet, if it is necessary to export its non-confidential information to the internet for analysis under special circumstances, manual copying of the optical disc will be adopted. Given the strict security control requirement of the computer room, a high degree of security for the confidential intranet data should be maintained.

The basic platform layer, constructed on the infrastructure, can implement all kinds of real-time processing of massive data and support a full range of service data processing scenarios such as data integration, stream data processing, transaction processing, online analysis, offline analysis, data mining, Etc. The basic platform layer provides a complete data acquisition system, as well as the whole distributed data storage mode, which can quickly build an information processing system for massive data. The basic platform layer can initiate unified data collection, high-performance data computation, intelligent data analysis, and diversified application support. The basic platform layer should meet the following needs:

- The first is the requirement for data. The internal data of regulators mainly consists of structured data, while the external data includes structured, unstructured, and semi-structured data. Therefore, the construction of the basic Platform should focus on ensuring comprehensive coverage and efficient support for various data types.
- The second is to analyze the demand. The data analysis services of the regulators include not only OLAP statistical analysis but also advanced AI algorithms.

Different types of data and analysis require different data processing engines and AI algorithms.

- The third is users' needs. The upper-layer users of the Big Data platform are the users of the analysis centers. Because each analysis center corresponds to a different regulatory domain and belongs to a different organization, the users should be managed as a whole in the basic platform layer.
- The fourth is high availability. Since Big Data platform bears a considerable amount of data, their high availability shows excellent importance. Therefore, the basic platform layer should use a mature, stable architecture to ensure that the business's development will not be affected when a failure occurs. The construction of the basic platform layer includes a data acquisition platform, a data storage platform, and a data analysis platform.

It is essential to construct a flexible and efficient data acquisition platform, which can provide a flexible, efficient, and extensible system capable of storing data across institutions for data loading, synchronization, and migration. The Platform can provide a complete/incremental and real-time/asynchronous data integration channel for dozens of data sources. However, the data acquisition platform should favor loading and synchronization operations for multiple data sources. The data acquisition platform realizes real-time access to mainstream relational and non-relational databases and streaming loading through seamless integration with distributed messaging systems. Also, the Platform provides standard access service interfaces for external application systems as well as file export and real-time writing services to business systems. Data acquisition can be carried out by user upload, API upload, streaming loading, batch file loading, real-time synchronization of relational databases, web crawler, API access, file export, real-time writing, etc.

The data acquisition platform supports data cleaning for the acquired data, which is to initiate consistency operations for different data types, such as format conversion, dirty data processing, format unification, Etc. The data cleaning process simultaneously completes various kinds of work such as secondary and primary key generation (all other fields except the primary key are calculated with a check value as a new field), data de-duplication (only one piece of data with the same primary key is retained), character encoding conversion (different character sets of different source systems need to be converted to a unified character set), Etc. In that case, data consistency can be ensured, and a massive heterogeneous data storage platform can be established. The data storage platform (data lake) is responsible for storing the raw data acquired by the data acquisition platform and preprocessing these data provided to the upper data warehouse. The data stored therein includes structured, semi-structured, and unstructured data, so it must have complete data storage and preprocessing capabilities. These raw data mainly include original ecological data such as internal data of the securities sector, external data, and internet data. After the preprocessing step of the data lake, these raw data are transformed into schema data that can be classified and used in the upper data warehouse and transmitted to the next upper data warehouse. It is crucial to establish panoramic and diverse data warehouses, data marts, and data analysis platforms based on the data storage platforms. Through the basic rules defined by the data model, all the data preprocessed by the data lake are constantly superimposed to produce panoramic analysis data. Data mining and analysis are mainly performed from the data warehouse, and the results of the mining and analysis can be migrated to the data mart for thematic analysis. Data mart is a special analysis processing oriented to themes or departments, which is a subset of data aggregated and filtered from the data warehouse according to the analysis requirements of the analysis center. The main capabilities of a data mart include supporting themes or department analysis requirements, user management, security management, log management, and operation management, and supporting data mutual access requirements among different data marts.

It is vital to notice the relationship between a data mart and a data catalog service. A data catalog is a component of the data processing platform that provides metadata and data services for sharing data among data marts. By registering metadata information of a data mart table in the data catalog service, other data marts can easily access and communicate them among data marts through the data catalog service. The data analysis platform uses various data types in data warehouses and marts. It utilizes various analysis tools provided by the Platform to initiate data analysis essential services. Each regulator should develop a data analysis platform in light of the situation.

8.3.3 China's Good Practice for Establishing Promotion Mechanism for SupTech

8.3.3.1 Overall Development Principles for the SupTech System and Mechanism

The PBOC is responsible for the overall management of the development and implementation of SupTech and coordinating and managing the collection, storage, processing, use, and sharing of data resources of the whole financial system. It also has the right to decide the scope and data-sharing methods. Various business departments of the PBOC, as the primary department, law-based administration, and routine supervision, actively utilize technical methods to solve practical problems. That being said, applying SupTech can be the necessary safeguard for these departments to perform their duties under the law. In the process of the development of SupTech, various regulators should, because of their regulatory work, put forward their specific business needs, the quality of which represents the level of the regulators.

Relevant financial regulators and regulated institutions, as participants in the development of SupTech, should undertake the responsibility and obligation of collecting all data resources generated and collected in the regulatory process into the central database as required by the development of SupTech. Data management should follow the guiding ideology: "data sharing is normal; non-sharing is an exception." However, data needed for the development of SupTech should be shared in principle (Zhang 2017).

8.3.3.2 Establishing a Management Mechanism for SupTech

- Communication and coordination mechanism

Under the unified leadership and organization of the Financial Stability and Development Committee of the State Council, the FinTech Committee of the PBOC will take the lead in establishing a communication and coordination mechanism with joint participation and equal dialogue of various parties, including academia, financial regulators, regulated financial institutions, and tech companies, to encourage the development of SupTech comprehensively.

- Organizational management mechanism

A well-functioning organizational structure should be established based on the development and coordination working group of SupTech, which includes several functions such as business requirements management, task analysis management, analysis center management, analysis result evaluation, examination of science and technology application, technology management, operation and maintenance management, and security and confidentiality management, to manage the whole life cycle of data analysis services effectively.

- Requirements review mechanism

The FinTech Committee of the PBOC, for the SupTech needs raised by its business departments, needs to formulate evaluation standards and strictly control the quality of such needs. First, however, the committee organizes relevant experts to demonstrate the needs proposed by various departments in the development of SupTech and evaluates the advancement. After that, the practicability and inclusiveness of business requirements should be assessed, and the decision on whether to initiate follow-up implementation based on the evaluation results should be determined.

- Data collection mechanism

The FinTech Committee of the PBOC, upon coordination and management of data processing, will formulate a data collection management system and coordinate with various departments and entities to prepare catalogs of data resources. Furthermore, they should supervise all nodes in the whole process of data collection and control the quality of data collection, and then establish a continuous and smooth data collection mechanism.

- Data sharing mechanism

The FinTech Committee of the PBOC coordinates and manages data sharing, formulates data sharing and desensitization systems, and implements standards to manage various types of data hierarchically. It should specify which kinds of data can be shared throughout the system, which kinds of data can be shared with specific objects, also which kinds of data need to be shared after desensitization. However, it should coordinate and manage the authority of the data used by the analysis centers and form a closed loop of data collection and sharing based on the application scenarios. It is essential to develop desensitization rules and supervise the desensitization implementation of projects.

- Mining analysis mechanism

Data mining and data analysis are essential components of SupTech. Therefore, it is crucial to regard data mining and data analysis as essential research topics, jointly formulate methods and models to complete data mining and analysis, assign tasks to relevant departments and entities based on business needs, and complete data analysis and mining in collaboration.

- Outcome feedback mechanism

It is crucial to evaluate the outcomes formed under SupTech programs and, by sharing among various regulators and business departments thereof, feedback on the good practice to regulators as a reference for their supervision work. A mechanism of task proposal, distribution, implementation, service provision, and outcome feedback should be established to ensure the efficient use of the outcomes of Big Data analysis services.

- Outcome evaluation mechanism

It is essential to clarify the standards and requirements of applying SupTech. The outcomes and performance of various data analysis services of SupTech should be evaluated, and the role of data analysis services in supporting regulatory work by indicators should be objectively measured, such as the breadth and depth of the application of data analysis services and application effects. Efforts should also be made to continuously deepen the application of effective services, and the services with less efficiency should be continuously improved.

- Application evaluation mechanism

It is significant to study and propose the standards and requirements for applying SupTech. The technical methods that the competent departments must adopt in exercising power and the SupTech supporting materials that must be provided for essential approval links should be clarified. The relevant departments should be evaluated according to whether such business departments have applied SupTech in their regulatory work and the application degree and level, which can incentivize regulators to improve the willingness and ability to apply SupTech continuously.

- Technology sharing mechanism

It is crucial to uniformly collect and manage the technologies, algorithms, and models used in various data analysis services and formulate working methods and workflow for technology sharing. Furthermore, a cooperation model for a technological breakthrough should be established to promote the implementation of various types of data analysis services in joint efforts.

- Technology innovation mechanism

It is vital to establish a mechanism for tracking, practicing, and applying new technologies, initiate a practical evaluation of new information technologies and intensify the application of those values to be used by SupTech. Technological breakthrough project teams should be formed to study various new technologies and new methods and promote the development of data analysis services based on advanced information technologies.

- External cooperation mechanism

It is important to intensify cooperation with different units and invite experts from relevant tech companies, universities, and scientific research institutions to participate in the construction of SupTech. Meanwhile, "extended brain" should be fully utilized to suggest SupTech. It is also essential for regulators to actively cooperate with relevant institutions and enterprises by inputting capacity and purchasing data and services so as to jointly promote the practice and application of SupTech in financial regulation.

- Security and confidentiality mechanism

It is significant to effectively manage the security and confidentiality of the regulatory Big Data platform and analysis results thereof, including system-level security, application-level security, data-level security, and other aspects. It is also critical to initiate hierarchical management of data, especially for the more sensitive data information in the Platform, and establish a security and confidentiality system from bottom to top (Sun 2019b).

References

Fu X, Liu Y (2018) Building a central bank decision-making platform to help digital central bank construction. Finance Electronization 6

Guofeng S (2019) Local financial supervision in the era of financial technology. China Financial Publishing House

Ningbo Radio and Television Network. Five major functions to prevent and control financial risks Ningbo to build Tianluo network monitoring and control system. http://www.nbtv.cn/xwdsg/nb/30031603.shtml

Sun G (2019a) China regulatory science and technology development report. Social Publishing House

Sun G (2019b) Research and practice of regulatory technology. China Finance Press

Sun G (2020) China regulatory science and technology development report. Social Publishing House

The Science and Technology Department of the People's Bank of China. Nanning branch independently developed a metadata management system to promote the construction of big data platform and the continuous development of data management and control. http://www.pbc.gov.cn/kejisi/146812/146814/3791642/index.html

Xuewen H (2019) Vigorously develop regulatory technology to help local financial supervision. Tsinghua Financ Rev 5

Zhang R (2017) Build a central bank decision-making platform supported by big data. Financial Electronization 5

Zhao D(2019) Ability and inability of RegTech. Tsinghua Financ Rev 5

Chapter 9
Policy Suggestions for SupTech Development

Introduction

Based on the history of financial supervision in China, in the past, financial regulators showed relatively high tolerance and low punishment for violations by financial institutions. Therefore, in that period, there had been no powerful outer driver and inner willingness to develop SupTech. However, in recent years, the Communist Party of China (the "CPC") and the Chinese government are attaching increasing importance to national financial security and financial risk prevention. As a result, the regulatory pressure faced by Chinese financial regulators is rising, and so is the importance of SupTech. Given this, Chinese financial regulators have put SupTech development on their agendas. Moreover, establishing and developing a solid SupTech regime can help improve the level and efficiency of financial regulation in China (Sun 2017).

9.1 Top-Level Design

It is essential to intensify the top-level design for the development of SupTech. The formulation of SupTech development plans and outlines in line with the existing financial regulation of China should be accelerated. In addition, the top-level design could include the guiding ideology, basic principles, goals and objectives, critical tasks, and safeguard measures to provide high-level guidance for further detailed policies.

From the perspective of national strategy, China comprehensively strengthens the research and application of SupTech and properly makes overall planning, strategic deployment, and supporting measures for SupTech, based on actual Chinese status and expectations on the new development trends of financial regulation in the future.

Balancing the innovation and risks of SupTech is one of the key topics in China's top level design. A delicate balance between innovation and risk control, will not only fully indicate the positive attitude of financial regulators towards the innovation but

D. Zhao et al., *FinTech and SupTech in China*, Contributions to Finance and Accounting,
https://doi.org/10.1007/978-981-99-5173-4_9

also keep the potential risks arising from the application of science and technology in the field of financial regulation within a controllable and reasonable range.

Top-level design can also guide achieving consistency between regulatory philosophy and regulatory methods. Keeping the development of SupTech in line with the regulatory philosophy of professionalism, consistency, and penetration is of significance. The innovation and transformation of regulatory methods should focus on the regulatory philosophy. The basic rules and system for the development of SupTech should be established and improved, with the standards, operation monitoring, and evaluation promoted simultaneously to explore a sound management mechanism for the innovation of SupTech.

Last but not least, it is essential to consolidate the fundamental supports of SupTech in the top-level design. A benign ecological environment for the development of SupTech should be explored and improved. The sustainable and orderly development of SupTech can only live with comprehensive guidance and support from the following aspects: regulatory logic, technology selection, standards and specifications, capital guarantee, academic support, and sector-university-research cooperation (Sun 2019a).

9.2 Standardize Technology Application in Financial Regulation

In general, applying technology in financial regulation is beneficial to improve efficiency and reduce the cost of financial regulation (Xu et al. 2017). However, multiple potential risks may hide in deploying technologies in financial regulation. At the same time, the practical application of technology in financial regulation should be smooth, with priorities given to the most concerned issues and problems in financial regulation. Furthermore, since technologies such as Big Data, Cloud Computing, AI, and Blockchain are still immature and have been leveraged by financial regulators for only a short time, it is still uncertain whether they will reduce the effectiveness of the current financial regulation or even bring new risks (Zhao 2019). Because of this, it is necessary to standardize the relevant processes and links in deploying new technologies in financial regulation by taking the following steps.

- First, ensure that the deployment of new technologies is compatible with the existing technical system of financial regulation and will not produce a substantially adverse impact on it.
- Second, ensure the consistency and continuity of financial regulation, with the basic principles and direction of regulation should remain the same under the application of new technologies.
- Third, establish a real-time monitoring, evaluating, and upgrading mechanism for SupTech and assess technology's role in financial regulation, aiming at adjusting, correcting, optimizing, and upgrading SupTech promptly.

- Last, regulate the R&D and application of key and general technologies and follow up on the infrastructure, technological selection, application arrangement, upgrading, safety control, etc. The goal is to enable SupTech to become the "roll booster" for improving the level and efficiency of financial regulation (Zhao 2021).

9.3 Conduct Comprehensive Research on SupTech

Regulators need to initiate a series of research on SupTech standards. It is indispensable to formulate standards and norms when developing SupTech. To provide a healthy and orderly ecological environment for the development of the regulatory industry, complete, unified, and transparent standards and norms of SupTech should be formulated. It is also necessary to formulate the R&D and application standards of SupTech, covering data collection, data analysis, data interaction, technology selection, technology planning, and technology assessment. Moreover, it will be helpful to learn from and participate in formulating the international standards of SupTech through international cooperation to lay the foundation for the "introduction" and "going global" of SupTech.

It is essential to research the docking system of SupTech. The ultimate goal of deploying SupTech is to prevent financial risks, ensure financial institutions' sound operation, and protect financial consumers' rights and interests. Therefore, SupTech should be able to interface with the existing financial regulation activities. Technical departments of regulators are generally responsible for exploiting platforms, systems, and regulatory tools based on new technologies. In the process, these departments should explore digital and technological paths for regulatory instructions and tasks. In other words, financial regulatory requirements with "technological language" should be better expressed to improve the effectiveness of financial regulation further.

It is also important to explore the supporting mechanism of SupTech. In developing SupTech, financial regulators in the United Kingdom, the United States, Singapore, etc., have paid great attention to building the ecological environment for SupTech development. By introducing universities and research institutes to conduct academic research on regulatory data, risk and compliance, technology R&D, and consumer protection, these countries provide academic support for the development of SupTech for improving the level of financial regulation and introduce business training institutions to conduct SupTech personnel training to meet the needs of financial regulators and financial institutions with regard to SupTech talents. To go further, financial regulators should expand the attention and efforts to SupTech and intensify exchanges between the sector and academia through holding forums and conferences.

As known from the regulatory practices from various countries, financial regulators are not only focusing on the application of technology in the field of financial regulation but also paying close attention to the development of technology itself. As mentioned in previous chapters, modern information technologies such as Cloud Computing, Big Data, AI, and Blockchain are yet to mature. Therefore, financial regulators may put forward demands on the future development of new technologies from the perspective of financial regulation and embed the regulatory connotation into the technical structure so that the R&D and deployment of new technologies can be more in line with the actual regulatory needs and future development trends (Sun 2019b).

9.4 Trans-Department and Trans-Institution Cooperation

Developing and deploying SupTech is a systematic project. It is nearly impossible to rely on a single department or institution to form an effective regulatory joint force. In some developed countries, financial regulators may cooperate with other government departments to widely apply SupTech in financial risk prevention and consumer protection. Regarding trans-department and trans-institution cooperation, this book suggests the following measures (Zhou 2020).

Firstly, promote information sharing among departments and agencies. To form the "joint force of data," information sharing and communication mechanisms should be established by integrating massive institutional and unstructured data. After that, it is possible to provide a broader database for Big Data analysis and AI decisions and boost the reliability of SupTech.

Secondly, integrate the resources of technologies, talents, and funds. A good way is to establish a regulatory R&D collaboration mechanism with one or more leading department(s) taking the lead to organize relevant authorities and institutions to participate in solving critical problems in the field of financial regulation.

Thirdly, initiate or strengthen the cooperation between academia and the sector. At present, the development of technology is unprecedentedly accelerated. However, many fundamental and theoretical problems of SupTech still need to be clarified, and the theoretical research lags behind the practice of SupTech. Therefore, academia and sectors must carry out comprehensive cooperation in the field of SupTech research and application.

Fourthly, enhance international cooperation. Learning from others is a good and economical way to advance. Therefore, it is important to communicate and exchange with foreign financial regulators and international financial organizations in SupTech. This way, various countries' regulators can absorb the latest technology and ideas with each other, conduct transnational SupTech cooperation, and prevent international regulatory arbitrage (Sun and Zhao 2018).

9.5 Accelerating SupTech's Application in Crucial Regulatory Areas

Based on the practical experience of the United Kingdom, the United States, and Singapore, these countries actively support the application of new technologies in financial regulation. For example, the United Kingdom is promoting the effectiveness of financial regulation by encouraging the development of SupTech, encouraging, nurturing, and funding financial institutions to utilize new technologies to meet regulatory requirements, and using Big Data technology and software integration tools to reduce financial institutions' compliance costs.

In general, the ultimate goal of SupTech is to ensure that it serves the public interest and national interest and maintains the stability of financial markets. It is furthermore promoting financial innovation that supports the real economy. Therefore, some countries have gradually formed some consensual principles concerning FinTech and SupTech, such as "driven by technological innovation," "premised on consumer protection," "focusing on the development of inclusive finance," "focusing on risk prevention," "based on standards and norms," and "encouraging positive competition and cooperation among diversified entities."

Currently, China is in an essential stage of preventing and controlling financial risks. As a result, financial regulation faces higher, more, and stricter requirements. In this context, to win the battle of prevention and control of financial risks and effectively exert the critical role of SupTech in preventing financial risks and assisting in the building of a new financial ecology, it is necessary to prioritize the development of SupTech regime for critical areas or areas with significant risks, such as regulating shadow banks, combating illegal fund-raising, promoting financial inclusion, and enhancing financial consumer protection, etc (Sun 2020).

9.6 Improve the Pilot Regulatory Sandbox

The regulatory sandbox is a practical choice to cope with the potential risks arising from the application of new technologies in the field of financial regulation and effectively solve the safety and applicability issues of SupTech. Therefore, the application and deployment of SupTech should base on full demonstration and practical tests, which should be carried out based on the regulatory requirements within the framework of laws and regulations.

In the ever-changing financial market, SupTech, regulatory philosophy, regulatory needs, existing SupTech regime, and the operation of SupTech in the actual regulatory environment require adjustments from time to time, with the compatibility and comprehensiveness fully considered, to ensure the timely detection of technical weaknesses of SupTech.

Shortening the time requisite for SupTech innovation helps relieve the pressure faced by financial regulators as soon as possible since the upgrading of technical regulation methods can speed up accordingly. First, however, it is essential to verify whether there is a positive "chemical reaction" between SupTech and financial regulation work, such as preventing financial risks, ensuring financial institutions' stable and sound operation, and protecting the rights and interests of financial consumers.

Numerous risks and safety issues may arise from applying new technologies in financial regulation. Therefore, addressing these risks and issues is beneficial for financial regulators to assess the actual effects of SupTech. On this basis, it will be helpful to learn from the experience in the sandbox testing of SupTech and leverage it for promotion and replication to lay a foundation for the constant innovation and development of SupTech (Zhao and Li 2020).

References

Sun G (2017) From FinTech to RegTech. Tsinghua Financ Rev (5)

Sun G, Zhao D (2018) Challenge and breakthrough of regulatory technology, no 21. China Finance

Sun G (Feb 2019a) Golden nail: new coordinates for China's fintech transformation. CITIC Publishing Group

Sun G (Oct 2019b) China regulatory science and technology development report. Social Publishing House

Sun G (Oct 2020) China regulatory science and technology development report. Social Publishing House

Xu Z, Sun G, Yao Q (Jul 2017) Fintech: trends and regulation. China Financial Publishing House

Zhao D (2019) Ability and inability of RegTech. Tsinghua Financ Rev (5)

Zhao D, Li X (2020) Research on financial supervision under the background of FinTech on the perspective of RegTech, no 4. Zhejiang Finance

Zhao D, Li J (Apr 2021) Intelligent financial era. People's Daily Press

Zhou L (2020) Improve corporate governance and promote the high-quality development of joint-stock banks. Res Financ Superv (7)

MIX
Papier aus verantwortungsvollen Quellen
Paper from responsible sources
FSC® C105338

If you have any concerns about our products,
you can contact us on
ProductSafety@springernature.com

In case Publisher is established outside the EU,
the EU authorized representative is:
Springer Nature Customer Service Center GmbH
Europaplatz 3, 69115 Heidelberg, Germany

Printed by Libri Plureos GmbH
in Hamburg, Germany